T0215347

Unleash Core Data

Fetching Data, Migrating, and Maintaining Persistent Stores

Avi Tsadok

Apress®

Unleash Core Data: Fetching Data, Migrating, and Maintaining Persistent Stores

Avi Tsadok
Tel Mond, Israel

ISBN-13 (pbk): 978-1-4842-8210-6   ISBN-13 (electronic): 978-1-4842-8211-3
https://doi.org/10.1007/978-1-4842-8211-3

Managing Director, Apress Media LLC: Welmoed Spahr
Acquisitions Editor: Aaron Black
Development Editor: James Markham
Coordinating Editor: Jessica Vakili

Distributed to the book trade worldwide by Springer Science+Business Media New York, 1 NY Plaza, New York, NY 10004. Phone 1-800-SPRINGER, fax (201) 348-4505, e-mail orders-ny@ springer-sbm.com, or visit www.springeronline.com. Apress Media, LLC is a California LLC and the sole member (owner) is Springer Science + Business Media Finance Inc (SSBM Finance Inc). SSBM Finance Inc is a **Delaware** corporation.

For information on translations, please e-mail booktranslations@springernature.com; for reprint, paperback, or audio rights, please e-mail bookpermissions@springernature.com.

Apress titles may be purchased in bulk for academic, corporate, or promotional use. eBook versions and licenses are also available for most titles. For more information, reference our Print and eBook Bulk Sales web page at http://www.apress.com/bulk-sales.

Any source code or other supplementary material referenced by the author in this book is available to readers on GitHub. For more detailed information, please visit http://www.apress.com/source-code.

Printed on acid-free paper

The choice of writing on a vast subject such as Core Data is truly a fascinating journey. But, even that journey could not be achieved without the help of my close ones. Therefore, I would like to thank my family – my kids, Harel and Maya, and my loving wife, Tammy, who gave me the time and strength to sit down, investigate, dig, and write. Without your unconditional support, this book would not exist.

Table of Contents

About the Author

Avi Tsadok is an accomplished iOS developer with almost a decade of experience. He is currently the head of mobile development at Melio Payments, a leading payments app. He's also a regular contributor to "Better Programming" and has an active presence on Medium. Having written many iOS articles, he's decided to combine his passion for writing and developing by writing his third book, along with "Pro iOS Testing" and "Mastering Swift Package Manager".

About the Technical Reviewer

Felipe Laso is a senior systems engineer working at Lextech Global Services. He's also an aspiring game designer/programmer. You can follow him on Twitter at @iFeliLM or on his blog.

CHAPTER 1

Welcome to Core Data

Nothing has ever been achieved by the person who says, "It can't be done."

—Eleanor Roosevelt

How I Met Core Data

Years ago, when I made my first steps in iOS development, I remember how I bumped into Core Data for the first time.

I also remember how immature iOS development was. No ARC, Auto Layout wasn't out yet, and Xcode was still a multiple-window IDE with iOS SDK version 3 as the most recent deployment version.

But I still remember the feeling I had. I was fascinated by how simple it was to use Core Data.

No SQL queries. No complicated setup or looping the SELECT results.

Core Data felt like magic, as if the data was "just there" when I needed it and in the format I needed.

But after a while, issues came up.

Weird crashes, concurrency issues, performance, migrations, and complicated predicates.

What I didn't know was that these issues weren't only my problem.

© Avi Tsadok 2022
A. Tsadok, *Unleash Core Data*, https://doi.org/10.1007/978-1-4842-8211-3_1

Stack Overflow and Apple Developer Forums were full of complaints and frustrated users.

After years of development, I understood something about Core Data – it's one of the most sophisticated, intelligent, and essential frameworks in iOS SDK. And while Core Data looks simple at first glance, it hides many secrets underneath we need to unleash to use it right.

That's why I called my book *Unleash Core Data*.

Why Is Core Data So Important?

Why did I choose to devote a whole book just to talking about managing a data store?

There are a couple of reasons.

Because It Defines Your Business

A standard application has three primary layers – UI, business logic, and data layer.

In most cases, our data structure is a refined representation of our app business.

Think about it – our data structure defines not only the main entities our app deals with but also their relationships with each other.

Also, the data structure is often optimized for our UI usage.

So you can derive from what I'm saying that your data layer is the foundation of your app. UI is important, but it is nothing without the data underneath.

And dealing with your data layer is like touching the core of your business. It's a fascinating world!

Because It Holds User Data

Your local data store is the soul of your app. When you think of your app architecture, your data layer is the only one that isn't static and gets filled as your app usage grows.

It looks different from one user to another and holds the user's most private data.

Music apps contain the user library. To-do apps have the user's personal tasks, and word processing apps include the user's personal documents.

And because of that reason, the data layer is so important. A problem with the UI layer may cause a weird experience on the screen. But a problem with the data layer can be devastating.

Because That's What We Sync

Many mobile apps that use a local store eventually sync their data to a backend server.

So the data isn't just the "structure of your business." It's also what we need to send out from the app and keep in the cloud.

The structure and behavior of our store need to consider a backend server at the end of the road, and that's another dynamic dimension of what Core Data is.

As a layer that is bound to the UI on one side and linked to your back end on the other side, Core Data plays a crucial role in your app architecture.

A Little Bit About Core Data History

Starting to talk about Core Data is like starting from the end. First, we need to understand the problem Core Data was trying to solve, and in doing that, we need to go back to the beginning, back then in the early 1990s. (Yes! 30 years ago.)

Object-oriented programming has existed for decades, but only in the early 1990s has it become the dominant programming paradigm for most developers.

But working with objects created a problem – SQL databases work in a two-dimensional data structure.

What developers had to do (and still need to) is to convert query results from tables to objects and vice versa – insert multidimensional objects into a two-dimensional data structure.

Look at Figure 1-1.

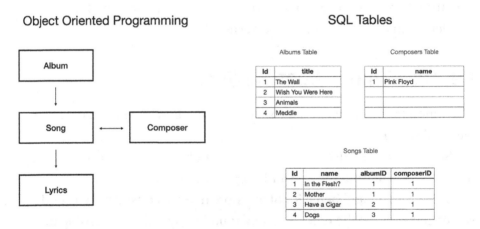

Figure 1-1. *Object-oriented programming vs. SQL tables*

You can see entities and their connections on your left, and on the right, you can see the same structure in SQL tables.

NeXT and Enterprise Objects Framework

The problem that appeared in Figure 1-1 was the leading cause the engineers in NeXT sat down and thought about what to do.

If you don't know what NeXT is, NeXT was a company founded in the late 1980s by Steve Jobs and later was purchased by Apple.

NeXT also developed NeXTSTEP – an OS that was the foundation for OS X and iOS.

By the way, NeXTSTEP initials are NS – that's why many classes in the Objective-C Foundation Framework have the prefix "NS," because they were part of NeXTSTEP OS.

NeXT developed a framework called "Enterprise Objects Framework" (EOF), which was supposed to solve the problem of writing SQL statements and mapping their results to objects.

EOF worked with both Java and Objective-C and was used to abstract the low-level data format and allow it to be based on non-SQL stores.

Note   A small anecdote – NeXT had a tiny engineering group that worked on EOF. One of them is Craig Federighi, today's Apple's SVP of Software Engineering.

In the late 1990s, NeXT turned EOF into a mature framework and made it the core of WebObjects, its application server.

Core Data Was Born

In 2000, Apple as the NeXT owner dropped support for EOF and discontinued the project.

When Apple launched "Cocoa," their OOP interface, they included Core Data and two other frameworks – Foundation Kit and Application Kit.

Core Data was a new framework, but some of its code was based on EOF Objective-C code.

At last, Core Data was introduced in WWDC 2004 as part of macOS Tiger, and later it was also added to iOS SDK 3.0.

From the beginning, Core Data was feature-rich. It had support for computed queries, properties, automatic undo support, deletion rules, etc.

All of these will be discussed in this book, but I wanted to state that regardless of its advanced features, Core Data is not new but rather a robust framework used by millions of applications, both iOS and Mac.

And looking even further, the code and the design start even earlier, in the NeXT company.

What Will You Learn in This Book?

Let's clarify something – this book **is not** technical documentation or a "how-to" tutorial.

The World Wide Web is full of tutorials and documentation, and probably, by the time you are reading this book, the material is even more updated.

I have no intention of competing with updated online information.

But what I do want to show you are

- The **methodology** of designing a good data scheme.

- How to **integrate a data layer** in a modern app architecture.

- How to work with Core Data in the **right way**. Methods and class names can change, but the fundamental way of using Core Data hasn't been changed for years. Design patterns can help you get things done more efficiently and fast.

This book is not a bunch of tutorials gripped together but rather a whole package of deep understating of what Core Data is.

Should You Be Using Core Data?

I think that's a critical question.

Core Data can be used for any app that **requires a complex data model**. Notice I didn't say "a local storage," because local storage is not the primary goal of Core Data.

If you need local storage, there are many options – user defaults, JSON files, or a local SQLite store.

The added value of Core Data is not the ability to manage a persistent store but to **provide a complete solution to manage your app data layer** above an optional persistent store.

If your app has different data models logically linked to each other, Core Data is for you.

Most apps have a "complex data model" – to-do, music, photos, word processing, email clients, calendars, tourism, etc.

Chapter 3 will discuss how to design a data model while looking at different app examples, so don't worry if that term might sound frightening to you.

How to Read This Book?

The book assumes you have very little knowledge (if any) about Core Data. Therefore, it is recommended to read all the chapters **in their order**.

But there are some advanced chapters that even the most experienced Core Data developers can find interesting. So, if you already have some knowledge about Core Data and are using it today in your projects, feel free to skip the first chapters and jump to a chapter you find interesting. That is perfectly fine!

Let's Begin!

Writing this book helped me establish a clear opinion about some Core Data aspects, and it also revealed many secrets I didn't know before.

Now it's time to unleash Core Data.

CHAPTER 2

Core Data Basics and Setup

Code is not like other how-computers-work books. It doesn't have big color illustrations of disk drives with arrows showing how the data sweeps into the computer. Code has no drawings of trains carrying a cargo of zeros and ones. Metaphors and similes are wonderful literary devices but they do nothing but obscure the beauty of technology.

—Charles Petzold

Like any other good design, we need to start with infrastructure to understand Core Data and create a good setup process.

Many developers are concerned about the Core Data setup process – mainly because they do not understand the different terms, how Core Data is built, and the several ways we have to approach it. Even senior developers sometimes look at Core Data with glazed eyes.

Hopefully, I'll try to clear things up.

In this chapter, we'll talk about

- What is Core Data

- What is the Core Data stack and why do we call it that way

© Avi Tsadok 2022
A. Tsadok, *Unleash Core Data*, https://doi.org/10.1007/978-1-4842-8211-3_2

- The different parts of the Core Data stack and how to initialize them

- How the persistent container can short things up for us

- How Xcode generates the stack for us and what we can learn from it

Let's jump in together.

What Exactly Is Core Data?

Before we set up our Core Data infrastructure and explore its wonders, we must start our journey with the expected one-million-dollar question – what is Core Data?

According to Apple

> *Use Core Data to save your application's permanent data for offline use, to cache temporary data, and to add undo functionality to your app on a single device. To sync data across multiple devices in a single iCloud account, Core Data automatically mirrors your schema to a CloudKit container.*

—Apple Documentation

Unlike what many developers think, Core Data **is not** a "Sqlite3 wrapper" or a "Sqlite3 replacement." When we think of a Sqlite3 wrapper, we usually imagine a simplified and more abstract way to handle Sqlite3 queries and updates.

In Core Data, we don't use "SELECT" queries to retrieve database table rows, and we don't use "UPDATE" to modify them.

In fact, there are cases where our store is not even Sqlite3 based, and we won't even know that.

Sometimes, our store is not event persistent because Core Data is first and foremost an **object graph manager**.

Core Data is tightly connected to our app models. If XIB, SwiftUI, or Storyboards are the "V" in MVC/MVVM, then Core Data represents the "M" (the Model).

The Core Data Developer Experience

Just like our app users have "user experience," we the developers also have our own "developer experience."

Let's look at the following code:

```
func reloadSongs() {
        let album = CoreDataManager.shared.getAlbum(byID
        albumID : "myAlbumID")
        self.title = album.title
        self.songs = album.songs
        tableView.reloadData()
 }
```

The preceding code looks ridiculously simple. We load an album object from our database, and it already has a title and a songs list.

Now, even though it looks like an ideal code, it's not a pseudo code. This is how Core Data usage actually looks like at the end of the road – fetching the title, connecting the "songs" to the "album," and many more are all handled by the Core Data framework.

The Core Data Stack

To understand how all the preceding magic happens, we need to dive into what we call the "Core Data stack."

Intuitive thinking will lead us to the conclusion that Core Data needs several things:

- A model scheme that defines all the entities and their relationships

- A data store that holds the data itself

- An easy way to access the data

These are, in fact, the main three components that Core Data is built upon – the managed data model, the persistent store coordinator, and the managed object context.

Why "Stack"?

Let's continue with our intuitive thinking.

When we approach a database design, we first imagine the different entities and how they relate. Therefore, the starting point would probably be our **database scheme**.

After all, the data store is created based on how our data is structured. Hence, the data model is at the bottom of the stack.

Naturally, the data store comes on top of the data model, and right after that comes the managed object context, which lets us modify our data store (again, based on our data model).

Creating the Core Data Stack

If the "stack" concept sounds confusing, don't worry! We will build the Core Data stack together, step by step, and everything will be more straightforward.

First, let's create our "CoreDataStack" class that will hold all the different Core Data components.

Note   "CoreDataStack" is just an arbitrary name I chose for the sake of learning. It can be any name, and you can even put these components wherever you think it's logical.

```swift
import CoreData

final class CoreDataStack {

        // This part will be filled!
}
```

Let's get an overview of the different components and add them to our stack.

The Managed Data Model

Note   We have a whole chapter discussing the data model and all its features. This is a quick summary of what is a data model in Core Data.

Unlike Sqlite3, we don't build our scheme with tables and properties but with **entities** and **attributes**.

If we have a music app, entities can be "Albums," "Playlists," "Songs," and more.

Attributes can be "name," "duration," and "year."

Up until now, it sounds similar to tables in Sqlite3, so what's the catch?

The managed data model can also describe the relationships between those entities.

For example, "Album" and "Song" have a "one-to-many" relationship – an album (may) contains multiple songs, and every song appears in one album only (for the purpose of the discussion).

In Sqlite3, we probably want another field in the Songs table named "albumID" to connect it to its album. In Core Data, we define a specific relationship between the Album entity and the Song.

The relationship describes how the Album and the Song are related to each other.

This creates a logical attribute that can help Core Data be more intelligent in different operations such as fetching optimizations, entity deletions, and more.

Another notable thing about the managed data model is that the model is agnostic to the type of persistent store we will use. Remember? The data model is at the bottom of the stack, which means we haven't decided yet on what kind of persistent store we have.

Creating a Managed Data Model

Creating a new managed data model is probably an action you will do once in your app development life cycle, and it's pretty simple, actually.

Go to your Xcode top menu and select File ➤ New ➤ File. In the opened window, you'll see a dedicated section for Core Data. (See? This is how essential Core Data is for developers [Figure 2-1].)

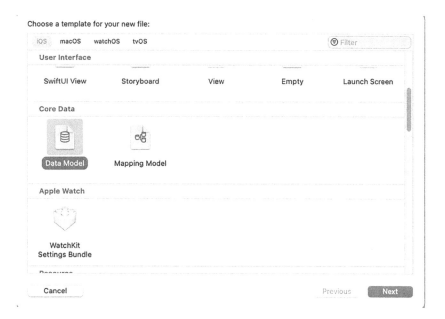

Figure 2-1. *Choosing the Data Model template*

True for Xcode 13, there are two available templates in the Core Data section – Data Model and Mapping Model (Figure 2-1). We are going to choose Data Model and continue.

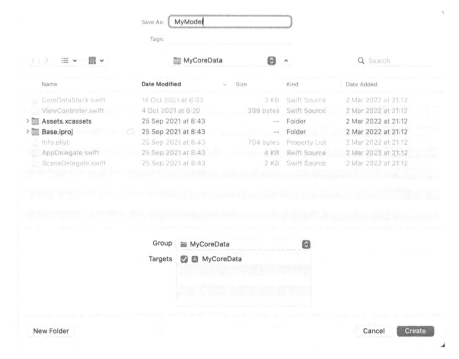

Figure 2-2. *Adding the xcdatamodeld file*

In the save file dialog window (Figure 2-2), select the relevant target location and create your new managed data model.

Tapping on the new file in Xcode reveals a UI that helps you manage your data types and custom fetch requests (Figure 2-3).

Figure 2-3. *Data model editor*

I don't want to get into details on how to design your data model; after all, we've got a whole chapter for that fun part. Nevertheless, I want to explain in general what we see in the file we've just created.

The managed data model file describes the different entities we will use and how we will fetch them into our memory.

We also describe how the entities are being linked to each other.

If we go back to our music app example, entities can be Song, Album, or Playlist.

We also know that Song and Album are linked together – every Song is linked to an Album, and an Album can be linked to multiple songs.

As mentioned earlier, this is our first step in creating the stack, but we can modify it later, carefully, as it influences our persistent store and our code.

Add the Managed Object Model to Our Stack

Our data model is represented by a class named NSManagedObjectModel.

To create an instance of this class, we need to initialize it with a URL of our model file we created earlier ("MyModel"):

```
private lazy var managedObjectModel: NSManagedObjectModel = {
        guard let url = Bundle.main.url(forResource: "MyModel",
        withExtension: "momd") else {
            fatalError("Unable to Find Data Model")
        }

        guard let managedObjectModel = NSManagedObjectModel
        (contentsOf: url) else {
            fatalError("Unable to Load Data Model")
        }

        return managedObjectModel
    }()
```

This is a straightforward code, right?

At first, we get the model file URL (notice its extension is momd), and then we initialize the object model while passing the model file URL.

We just created the first layer of our stack. Kudos to us!

Let's move on to the persistent store.

The Persistent Store

As its name indicates, the persistent store is the place where Core Data saves our objects.

Whenever we create a new entity or modify an existing one, at the end of the road, the data is being saved in our persistent store.

There are several store types we can choose from. However, not all of them are available on all platforms.

Four Store Types

Apple provides us with four different store types – one in memory and three saved on the disk.

Chances are that the only time you are going to "touch" the persistent store is when you set your Core Data stack, but even then, you should be familiar with the different types to get a broader perspective on how Core Data works underneath.

In Memory

The in-memory store type is a unique one because it's not a persistent store. Core Data objects behave as usual in this type, but they vanish the minute your application is killed.

If you currently ask yourself, "Why would I use an in-memory store? I don't see a point for that action," you probably misunderstood what Core Data is.

Core Data is not a "database." It's an "object graph and persistent framework."

First and foremost, it's a framework that helps you maintain your objects' relationships. Its additional feature is to save those objects and their relationships to disk.

This means that persistent storage is an **optional** feature of Core Data!

In-memory stores are being used when we want to maintain a temporary graph of objects. For example, we can use the in-memory store type to hold a binary tree or a trie.

You could use it to hold complex data received from an HTTP request.

Try to think more comprehensively than just a database – Core Data can solve problems in different areas rather than being just a persistent store.

Another everyday use case of an in-memory store is unit and integration tests.

The first step in unit tests is data preparation. There's no need to read and write to a local store file using the in-memory store type. Working with the in-memory store type prevents many issues like working with an existing DB file with running app data or running concurrent tests using the same persistent file.

Let's add together another lazy-loading variable to our Core Data stack that creates an in-memory store:

```
private lazy var persistentStoreCoordinator:
NSPersistentStoreCoordinator = {
        let persistentStoreCoordinator = NSPersistentStoreCoord
        inator(managedObjectModel: self.managedObjectModel)

        do {
            try persistentStoreCoordinator.
            addPersistentStore(ofType: NSInMemoryStoreType,
                                        configurationName: nil,
                                        at: nil,
                                        options: nil)
        } catch {
            fatalError("Unable to Add In-Memory Store")
        }

        return persistentStoreCoordinator
    }()
```

The NSPersistentStoreCoordinator mission is to connect our object model to our store.

The coordinator doesn't give you direct access to the store – that's why it is called a "coordinator" and not a store.

When using the in-memory store type, all the "saved" data are gone when the app is killed.

For a persistent storage, we have better solutions, like a SQLite-based store.

SQLite

The SQLite store type is probably the most common store type used in Core Data.

Not only using the SQLite store type is fast but it's also the go-to option to be used on iOS platforms – the XML store type, for example, is not supported for iOS.

The SQLite option is also the most efficient store type in terms of memory – unlike the other options, Core Data does not need to hold the whole memory graph in memory. Core Data makes a SQLite query, parses the results, and keeps what's relevant in memory to make fetch requests.

The creation of a SQLite persistent store type is similar to the in-memory one – but in this case, we also need to pass a path for our SQLite file:

```swift
private lazy var persistentStoreCoordinator:
NSPersistentStoreCoordinator = {
        let persistentStoreCoordinator = NSPersistentStoreCoord
        inator(managedObjectModel: self.managedObjectModel)

        let fileManager = FileManager.default
        let storeName = "MyStorage.sqlite"
        let documentsDirectoryURL = fileManager.urls(for:
        .documentDirectory, in: .userDomainMask)[0]
        let persistentStoreURL = documentsDirectoryURL.appendin
        gPathComponent(storeName)

        do {
           let options = [
               NSMigratePersistentStoresAutomaticallyOption :
               true,
               NSInferMappingModelAutomaticallyOption : true
           ]
```

```
    try persistentStoreCoordinator.addPersistentStore
    (ofType: NSSQLiteStoreType, configurationName: nil,
    at: persistentStoreURL, options: options)

} catch {
    fatalError("Unable to Add Persistent Store")
}

    return persistentStoreCoordinator
}()
```

As I said, the main difference is that we need to provide a full path for our SQLite file this time. If the file doesn't exist, Core Data will create it for you.

The SQLite DB scheme is created based on the object model being passed to the coordinator.

What will happen if we change the object model after the SQLite DB file is already created? It sounds like it might cause significant drawbacks.

Well, it will, and your app might even crash. But Core Data has a solution for that, and we will discuss it later in this book.

As a developer, it's important not to make any modifications to the SQLite file itself. In fact, you don't need to touch it at all during your development process.

Core Data has its unique way of organizing your entities' data in tables, and the SQLite file is for the use of the Core Data framework only.

Binary and XML Store Types

I decided to put the last two store types together. First, because most of the apps choose the SQLite store type. And, second, because they share the same behaviors.

There are several differences between binary and XML store types:

1. XML is available on macOS only. This fact eliminates XML as the selected store type for most developers when most work on iOS versions.

2. XML is a readable format. Unlike SQLite, which uses its own structure, or binary, which is (almost) impossible to read, XML can be read and even edited by "humans." The XML store type can be great for debugging and investigations.

3. In a large amount of data, XML takes time to parse. This is the main reason XML is supported on macOS only. I agree that iOS devices are much more powerful now, but you should also remember that the user experience on iOS devices requires a much shorter waiting time and is more speedy than Macs.

If we go back to writing code (that's why we're here), to set up a binary or XML store type, all we need to do is change the `type` parameter in the `addPersistentStore` method and update the file name:

```
persistentStoreCoordinator.addPersistentStore(ofType:
NSXMLStoreType
```

The rest of the code can be left as it is.

23

Custom Store Type

What do we do when none of the provided store types work for us? For example, we already have a data file that we downloaded and want to use as our DB, but of course, the file structure is unique to our product. Or maybe we want to move to Core Data and don't want to migrate our existing app data.

Fortunately, we can create our own store type, subclassing NSIncrementalStore or NSAtomicStore.

Creating your own custom store is considered an advanced Core Data implementation, so we will get into more details of that later in this book.

At this stage, remember it exists so we can move forward with our journey!

The Context

Right now, our stack is built from a model and a data store. Our last piece is the **managed object context**.

The managed object context lies on top of the stack and serves as a scratch pad for most of our Core Data activity.

This is the place where we create, fetch, or modify our objects.

Why is it called a context?

A *context* often means "environment," which is precisely the usage of context in Core Data.

Any work with objects is relevant only to the specific context that we work on until we "save" it.

How do we create a context? Like this:

```
lazy var managedObjectContext: NSManagedObjectContext = {
    let managedObjectContext = NSManagedObjectContext(concurren
    cyType: .mainQueueConcurrencyType)
```

```
managedObjectContext.persistentStoreCoordinator = self.
persistentStoreCoordinator
```

```
return managedObjectContext
}()
```

The creation of a managed object context requires two major configurations.

The first one is the concurrency type. The concurrency type identifies the type of the created context in terms of, well, concurrency.

There are two types – main and private.

For the sake of the example, we created a context in the main queue only. But don't worry. We will learn how to deal with contexts in a multi-threading environment very shortly in this book so you can become a real Core Data ninja.

The second configuration is linking the new context to our persistent store:

```
managedObjectContext.persistentStoreCoordinator = self.
persistentStoreCoordinator
```

That's the same persistent store we created earlier, remember?

If you're a little bit confused about the term, that's okay. I assure you that understanding the Core Data stack is probably one of the most confusing parts of understanding Core Data in general. Let me help you lighten up the issue by looking at a small code snippet on how to create a new album entity, using our managed object context:

```
let album = NSEntityDescription.insertNewObjectForEntityForName
("Album", inManagedObjectContext: managedObjectContext)
```

That's it? Yes! It's only one line.

Remember, our context is on top of the stack, linked to our data model and the persistent store.

Later, we've got a whole chapter explaining how to write sophisticated stuff with contexts.

Core Data Container

A small secret – don't tell anyone, but I didn't invent the `CoreDataStack` class I just showed you. In fact, you can find it everywhere – in tutorials, books, and existing projects.

A few years ago, it was even created for you by Apple every time you started a new project from scratch and marked "Use Core Data" on the project setup.

I had to show you the Core Data stack to explain the different parts of the stack. Now that you (hopefully) understand it, I can reveal that Apple listened to developers and in iOS 10 created its own "CoreDataStack" class, named `NSPersistentContainer`. (Don't be confused with `NSPersistentStoreCoordinator`.)

How simple is it? Very. Let's have a look:

```
let container = NSPersistentContainer(name: "MyStore")
container.loadPersistentStores(completionHandler: {
(storeDescription, error) in }
```

Yes, two lines of code (if ignoring error handling) are more than enough to set up Core Data. The container has everything we need to move on with our code.

Accessing Context

If you remember, the context is probably the most used part in the Core Data stack. Accessing the Core Data container context is easy:

```
let context = persistentContainer.viewContext
```

Why is it called "`viewContext`"? Good question. Remember that context is used to handle our data in a multi-thread environment. It also means that every queue has its own context, and it's true for the main queue as well.

The `viewContext` belongs to the main queue, the one that also manages the UI. That's the reason the `viewContext` is called like that.

The container also has the ability to create a private context for you to be used on a background thread:

```
let privateContext = persistentContainer.newBackgroundContext()
```

Don't be nervous. If you don't know yet what to do with a private context, we have an entire chapter for that!

More Configurations

When we created our Core Data stack from scratch, you probably noticed that we had many choices and flexibility to perform changes. For example, we could set the store type or work with a specific data model.

It is true that when we use `NSPersistentContainer`, everything is done for us.

However, we can still configure our persistent container to our needs.

For example, we can initialize a container while passing a different name for the store file and the data model.

Instead of

```
let container = NSPersistentContainer(name: "MyStore")
```

we can do

```
    var objectModel: NSManagedObjectModel {
        guard let url = Bundle.main.url(forResource: "MyModel",
        withExtension: "momd") else {
            fatalError("Unable to Find Data Model")
        }

        guard let managedObjectModel = NSManagedObjectModel(con
        tentsOf: url) else {
```

```
            fatalError("Unable to Load Data Model")
        }
        return managedObjectModel
    }

    func persistentContainer() {
        let container = NSPersistentContainer(name:
        "mysqlFile", managedObjectModel: objectModel)
    }
```

NSPersistentContainer has an optional parameter for the object model. If not implemented, Core Data will look for a data model with the same name as the SQLite file.

We can also set a different store type, using NSPersistentStoreDescription, like this:

```
let container = NSPersistentContainer(name: "mysqlFile")
let storeType = NSPersistentStoreDescription()
storeType.type = NSInMemoryStoreType
container.persistentStoreDescriptions = [storeType]
```

If you think that moving to NSPersistentContainer decreases your modification capability, NSPersistentStoreDescription changes that picture.

There are many more configurations you can do using NSPersistentStoreDescription.

You can handle the migration type, set the store as read-only, control the timeout duration, or even execute a PRAGMA statement within the SQLite file.

In most cases, the "two-line" container setup I showed you at first is more than enough to get you started. Just remember that using the persistent container doesn't mean you gave up your freedom.

Let Apple Create the Container for Us

Even though creating the container/stack is probably a one-time task in our app development cycle, historically speaking, it is considered to be a "complicated" mission.

Apple understood that and created an automatic process that creates a stack for us when setting up a new project from scratch.

Look at Figure 2-4.

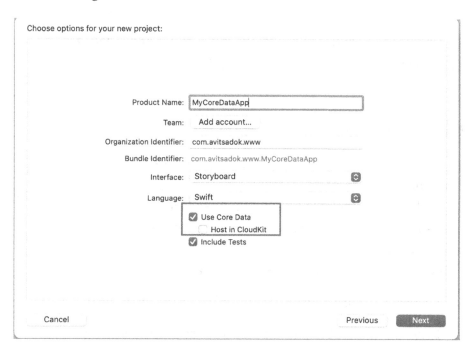

Figure 2-4. *Setting up a new project with Core Data*

The "new project options" dialog has a dedicated checkbox named "Use Core Data," followed by another checkbox named "Host in CloudKit."

CloudKit is a great feature that deserves its own chapter. Therefore, we will not discuss CloudKit now. Don't worry; the best things come to those who wait.

So what does the "Use Core Data" checkbox do? In short, it creates an NSPersistentContainer and helps you hold it as a Singleton in your app. The way Xcode does it is different between SwiftUI and UIKit.

Remember, the checkbox is only the initial setup Apple does for us, and we can always change or modify it later.

UIKit-Based App

In a UIKit-based app, the Xcode wizard uses the App Delegate to store the persistent container.

Xcode does it similar to what we discussed earlier in this chapter – it creates a lazy-loading variable that initializes the container (again, two lines!) and returns it:

It even adds comments and a pragma mark!

```
// MARK: - Core Data stack

lazy var persistentContainer: NSPersistentContainer = {
    /*
    The persistent container for the application. This
    implementation creates and returns a container, having
    loaded the store for the application to it. This
    property is optional since there are legitimate error
    conditions that could cause the creation of the store
    to fail.
```

```
*/
let container = NSPersistentContainer(name:
"MyCoreDataApp2")
container.loadPersistentStores(completionHandler: {
(storeDescription, error) in
    if let error = error as NSError? {
        // Replace this implementation with code to
        handle the error appropriately.
        // fatalError() causes the application to
        generate a crash log and terminate. You
        should not use this function in a shipping
        application, although it may be useful during
        development.

        /*
         Typical reasons for an error here include:
         * The parent directory does not exist, cannot
           be created, or disallows writing.
         * The persistent store is not accessible, due
           to permissions or data protection when the
           device is locked.
         * The device is out of space.
         * The store could not be migrated to the
           current model version.
         Check the error message to determine what the
         actual problem was.
         */
        fatalError("Unresolved error \(error), \(error.
        userInfo)")
    }
})
return container
}()
```

Notice Xcode also adds another method for saving your context changes.

Holding the container in the App Delegate is a decent solution, but in my opinion, it's not the best practice.

Don't be dazed by the fact that Apple chose to put the container in the App Delegate – even Apple is not perfect.

Apple chose to put the container in your App Delegate because we need one and only one instance of the Core Data container.

So what can be a better best practice?

One option would be to create your own Singleton that holds the container.

Many developers don't like Singletons, so the following solution can be dependency injection and passing the container along with the app.

An interim solution can be putting all the container logic in a separate class and letting the App Delegate hold an instance of that class.

No matter what you choose to do, try to keep the App Delegate clean as you can and reserve it mainly for system calls and events.

SwiftUI-Based App

Why do I explain about a SwiftUI-based app now? How does it relate to the Core Data stack?

SwiftUI is just another way to build UI. But the way the Xcode wizard builds the Core Data container for us is interesting when dealing with SwiftUI.

SwiftUI Uniqueness

Relax. We are still on the Core Data book here. But the Core Data framework lives in our app and aims to serve the UI.

Why is the container implementation different when we use SwiftUI?

Let's see. SwiftUI has two main differences compared with UIKit:

- There is no App Delegate. There is a struct conforming to the App protocol, and just like other structs that conform to View, the "app" **struct is immutable**.

- As part of the development process, SwiftUI views have something called Preview. Preview often requires mock data to be displayed. Since many SwiftUI views are linked to Core Data (another issue we need to discuss), **we can't use the data held by the persistent store**.

The two differences I just mentioned are the result of a different approach Apple took with SwiftUI.

Look at the following code snippet from the PersistentController automatically created by Xcode:

```
struct PersistenceController {
    static let shared = PersistenceController()

    static var preview: PersistenceController = {
        let result = PersistenceController(inMemory: true)
        let viewContext = result.container.viewContext
        for _ in 0..<10 {
            let newItem = Item(context: viewContext)
            newItem.timestamp = Date()
        }
..
}
```

First, we can see the PersistenceController is a struct, and it also has two static class instances: one (shared) for the use by the app and the other (preview) for the use of the different SwiftUI previews we depend on during the SwiftUI view development.

The preview instance is initialized with the inMemory parameter, set to true. This is how the init method looks like:

```
init(inMemory: Bool = false) {
        container = NSPersistentContainer(name:
        "MyCoreDataProject")
        if inMemory {
            container.persistentStoreDescriptions.first!.url =
            URL(fileURLWithPath: "/dev/null")
        }
```

So, unlike the "UIKit" version, the SwiftUI version seems much more elegant and valuable. Try it yourself!

Summary

In this chapter, we did an unbelievable step. We created our first Core Data infrastructure, and it wasn't even the fun part of the book!

We've learned about the different parts of the stack and how to create it from scratch, use the container, and even use the Xcode auto-generated version.

At this point, I encourage you to try it yourself – create a new project in Xcode, mark "Use Core Data," and see what happens.

In the next chapter, we'll start investigating and discovering our new stack, and we'll start with the most bottom layer – the data model.

CHAPTER 3

The Data Model

Where there is data smoke, there is business fire.

—Thomas Redman

In the previous chapter, we talked about the Core Data stack. That gave us a good overview of what Core Data is and how it's built.

Now it's time to start digging in!

The first stack layer is our data model – that's why we will start exploring there.

In this chapter, we'll talk about

- The Core Data model editor

- What are entities and how to add them

- What are attributes and what types of attributes do we have

- How to generate classes based on our entities

- How to configure the attributes to our needs

Let's start!

© Avi Tsadok 2022
A. Tsadok, *Unleash Core Data*, https://doi.org/10.1007/978-1-4842-8211-3_3

The Importance of the Core Data Model

The importance of your data model is undeniable. When you deeply think of it, the data model defines not only the lowest layer of your Core Data stack, but it's also the core of your app business logic!

Let's just focus on that for a second – your app is based on different data entities and how they relate to each other. This is what the data model is all about.

When you want to describe an app for someone, you can show them your data model – in most cases, that will work.

The Core Data Model Editor

In the previous chapter, we already created a data model, so you can go back and see what we did.

Let's try to examine what the Core Data model screen looks like in Xcode (Figure 3-1).

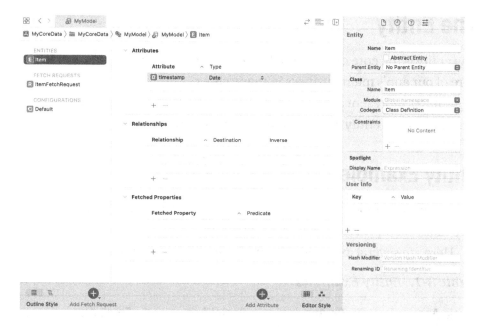

Figure 3-1. *Core Data model editor in Xcode*

We already saw the Core Data model editor in the previous chapter, but only briefly.

What the Core Data model editor does is help you **edit your Entities list**, define them, and add more configuration and built-in fetch requests. It is a powerful tool we have built-in in Xcode, and it's super helpful and accessible.

To understand how to work with the editor, we first need to understand what an entity is.

The Entity

The entity is the core of our model, and as mentioned before, it's also the core of our app's main business in many cases.

Entities represent a piece of data in our app. If we look back to our "music app," an entity can be an Album, a Song, or a Playlist.

Entity Examples

The entity is so important to our discussion that I want to continue and give more examples to be clear on that point.

Here are several examples for entities in different types of apps.

Table 3-1. *Entity Examples*

Music App	To-Do App	Social App	Email App
Album	List	Post	Account
Song	Task	Comment	Message
Playlist	Attachment	Reaction	Inbox

By looking at Table 3-1, you can see why I said we could describe our app business by looking at the data model. It's really at the center of our app idea.

Did Someone Say SQL Tables?

The first reaction to entities is to try and compare them to what we know from SQLite and see them as database tables.

But comparing entities to database tables is a typical mistake developers make when they first approach Core Data.

SQL tables contain various information in a tabular data set. It's true that for "Album," we may have a table named "Albums" (the same for songs and playlists).

But we also create tables for other needs. For example, to define many-to-many relationships between entities, we create a dedicated linking table.

We also create tables to expand other tables, to create views, computed data, and more.

But I think the main reason it's a mistake to look at entities as tables is the point of view.

Entities should be an explicit **and declarative representation** of our app's main idea. On the other hand, tables represent the implementation of these ideas.

Adding a New Entity

Adding a new entity is easy – just click "Add Entity" on the bottom of the editor or go to **Editor ➤ Add Entity**, and a new entity is added to the list.

To rename the new entity we just created, double-tap it, or select and rename its name in the text field on the right pane.

Notice that the entity must start with a capital letter – remember that at the end, the entity is represented in your code as a class, so starting with a capital letter is a standard naming convention.

Attributes

This is probably the fun part of the book.

What are attributes?

Thinking about SQL, attributes are like "columns," but they are much more than that.

When dealing with their code representation, attributes become class properties.

"name", "id", and "time" are typical attributes, and just like columns in SQL tables, they also have their own type.

Core Data supports 13 types of data. Of course, we have the typical suspects such as Text, Int, and Boolean, but we also have other interesting and valuable types like UUID, Date, and URI (look at Figure 3-2).

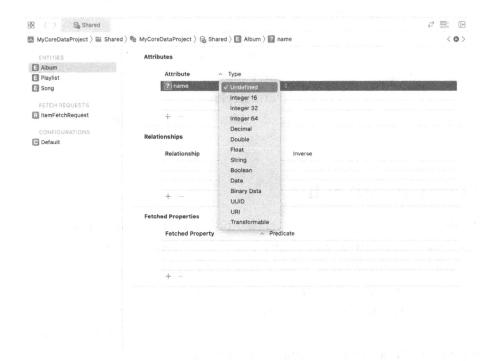

Figure 3-2. *Setting a type for an attribute*

Attribute Types

Let's talk about the different attribute types as it stands in the center of our data model design.

We can use many data types to identify our attributes, and in most if not all cases, this long list should fill your needs easily.

Looking at Figure 3-2, you can see the list of types – Integer 16, Decimal, String, Date, and more.

Let's go over some of them.

Number

I know that "Number" is too generic, but there are six types of "Number" in Core Data.

The first three are integers: Integer 16, 32, and 64. This is equivalent to Swift `int16`, `int32`, and `int64`.

If you have a massive amount of data, I recommend choosing wisely as it affects performance and storage.

Integer 16 – For numbers between –32,768 and 32,767

Integer 32 – For numbers between –2,147,483,648 and 2,147,483,647

Integer 64 – For numbers between –9,223,372,036,854,775,808 and 9,223,372,036,854,775,807

(You don't need to remember that, of course; there is no exam at the end of the book.)

The other three types are more attractive: `Double`, `Float,` and `Decimal`. `Float` is 32-bit, and `Double` is 64.

So why do we need the `Decimal` type? Don't `Float` and `Double` hold fractional numbers?

Look at the following code:

```
var sum: Float = 0.3 + 0.6
let result = (sum == 0.9) // return false!
```

(Unlike other experiments, you can safely try that at home.)

First, relax. You don't have a bug in your Xcode, so you don't need to reinstall it.

But perhaps not all readers are aware of the fact that `Float` and `Double` may result in inaccurate answers when trying to do math calculations or trying to test their values.

The reason is because of the challenge of storing fractional values.

For math calculations and accuracy, it is better to use Decimal.

This (modified) code will work just fine:

```
let decimalA = Decimal(floatLiteral: 0.3)
let decimalB = Decimal(floatLiteral: 0.6)
let sum = decimalA + decimalB
let result = (sum == 0.9) // result true
```

The downside of choosing Decimal is that Decimal variables **take 128 bits of storage**.

So, in the end, choosing the correct data type really depends on your needs. For finance apps, for example, it is better to work with Decimal data types.

Float and Double data types are suitable for storing values used on UI animation and painting, for example.

Like everything in life, it is all about **compromises and choices**.

String, Boolean, and Date

The following three types are more straightforward to use.

Let's start with String, and the first question often asked is, Does the String type have any length limit?

The answer is no. But remember that our Core Data stack is based on an actual data store.

The column type defined in SQLite for String attributes is VARCHAR. Even though we define a size for VARCHAR (VARCHAR(10)), it has no limits in practice.

Using Date and Boolean is simple as it sounds. Later, we'll see how these attribute types are being generated in code and how to configure them to our needs.

URI, UUID, and Binary Data

In theory, using String, Integer, and Float might fulfill all our needs. We can save almost anything we want using these data types. But Core Data is here to make our coding life more enjoyable and convenient, so why not just go with it?

In iOS 11, Apple added additional two data types – URI and UUID. The reason for that is obvious – URI (URL) is used in many entities to point to resources and network locations, and UUID is used almost in every client that has to deal with fetching data from a server.

So, even though we can use String to save URL addresses and IDs, URI and UUID provide us with a cleaner and more elegant way to store them.

Binary Data is a different story. This attribute type is used to store chunks of Data in our models. Binary Data is beneficial for saving things such as image information right inside our Core Data.

The first thing that pops into our mind is whether it hits our app performance and memory.

The answer (again) is it depends.

If our store type is in memory or XML, then, yes, you'll get a performance hit.

If you remember from our previous chapter, in-memory and XML store types require Core Data to load the entire data store to memory.

So loading an entity that stores an image means fully loading the image into our RAM!

Basing our data store on SQLite is much better, but the best practice is to store files in our file system and store a URL that points to that file.

Like many things in coding, separations are essential. Keeping the files in a different place is healthier and can give us more flexibility in the long run.

Transformable

What happens if we want to store data that is more complex than numbers and strings? For example, what if we're going to store not just a string but an array of strings?

The traditional way would be to convert it to a JSON and save it as one string:

```
["1", "2", "3"]
```

How about that? Aren't we creative today or what?

Well, that could work. But it doesn't seem to be an efficient way to store data. Think about more complex structures or objects. If we save a JSON that has keys and values, how do we handle type safety?

That's what the Transformable attribute type is for. We can set not only "primitive" types or types like Date or Data that we saw earlier but, basically, almost anything we like.

An array of strings is a classic example of Transformable usage, but we don't have to stop here – we can even store custom classes, as long as they conform to the NSCoding protocol.

To understand how to do that, we first need to know how entities are reflected in our code.

Generated Classes

We barely scratched the surface with everything related to entities and attributes, but don't worry – we'll get back to them later.

Now that we know how to create entities and attributes, the obvious question should be, How to use them in our code?

The short answer is to tell you that a class represents each entity and every attribute is a property, but that would be too easy and simple.

I want you to be a real Core Data master, so I'll explain how things are built underneath, as it is really, really neat.

How Is Your Data Model Really Created

I just explained to you that if you want to create a data model, you need to use the Core Data model editor, and that's true, but I have a secret – it's not the only way.

Using the Core Data model gives us the feeling that the data model is static and cannot be created in runtime.

But it's not true. Core Data is much more dynamic than you think. In fact, you can even create your whole data model, in runtime, straight from your code!

Want to see an example? Here you go:

```
let model = NSManagedObjectModel()

let album = NSEntityDescription()
album.name = "Album"
album.managedObjectClassName = "Album"

let titleAttribute = NSAttributeDescription()
titleAttribute.name = "Title"
titleAttribute.attributeType = .stringAttributeType

let properties = [titleAttribute]
album.properties = properties

model.entities = [album]
```

Without getting into too many details, the preceding code defines an Album entity with a Title attribute.

The preceding code practically replaces the model editor.

Defining your data model straight from code is not something I recommend, but I gave this example to show you that it's possible.

Wait. If it's not recommended, why am I telling you that?

Because that shows us that creating your data scheme is fully dynamic and not only can be done in runtime – this is precisely how it happens.

And that leads us to another interesting question. On the one hand, the data model is created dynamically. On the other hand, we have classes and properties that represent the same entities and attributes that weren't there when the app was compiled. How does it happen?

What Is NSEntityDescription?

Looking at our previous code snippet, you probably saw a class named NSEntityDescription.

To understand how the magic happens, we first need to explore what NSEntityDescription means.

The best way of doing that is to use an analogy from the SQL world. When we set up a SQL database, the first thing we do is create a table. Creating a table doesn't mean we create any entities – it just means we give the table its name and define its properties and their type.

In Core Data, NSEntityDescription is much like tables in SQLite (or "classes" in object-oriented programming) – it defines how our entities will look.

If we want to add another entity to our data model, we can just create NSEntityDescription, add new attributes, and append it to our data model, just like we did in the preceding example.

From the reverse direction, we can easily get the list of entity descriptions from the data model.

Look at the following code:

```
let entities : [NSEntityDescription] = PersistenceController.
shared.container.managedObjectModel.entities // get all
entity descriptions in our data model


let entity : NSEntityDescription = PersistenceController.
shared.container.managedObjectModel.entitiesByName["Album"]! //
get specific description
```

Now that we know that NSEntityDescription is like a "class" or a "table," what is the "instance" or "row" in our analogy?

The answer is NSManagedObject.

Welcome, NSManagedObject

You probably have a good reason if you are excited as I am (aren't you?).

NSManagedObject is our way to represent our data in code so we can read, update, and, on the bottom line, start using it.

NSManagedObject is a class that stores data from the Core Data store. Let's organize that in a diagram (Figure 3-3).

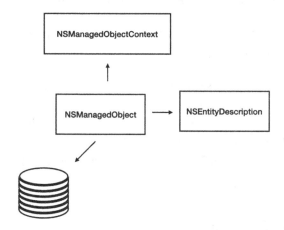

Figure 3-3. *NSManagedObject in the center*

If Figure 3-3 is not clear enough for you, I'll try to explain that and, on the way, summarize things up:

NSEntityDescription defines the name and the attributes entity.

NSManagedObject stores the data itself.

The **NSManagedObjectContext** tracks changes in your data.

Sounds much like classes, instances, and memory.

Access and Save Data

Try to think of NSManagedObject as a dictionary that holds keys (the attributes' names) and values.

To see the different attributes, we need to go to the description of the entity and look there:

```
let allAttributes = myAlbum.entity.attributesByName
```

Now, saving and reading values looks similar to a dictionary.
For instance, if we want to retrieve an album title, we can do

```
let title = myAlbum.value(forKey: "title") as? String
```

If Album doesn't have a title attribute, "title" will be nil.
Setting a new value is similar:

```
myAlbum.setValue("Dark Side of The Moon", forKey: "title")
```

Wait a second. This is all great, but the previous chapter's examples showed that entities like "Albums" can have a property named "title". Why do we need to use the setValue or valueForKey method and not approach straight to the property?

Managed Properties

We are in a weird situation here. First, I showed you that managed objects could have a "title" property. But then, I told you that attributes are always being added in runtime. How can we add properties **before** we know what the corresponding attributes are?

Here we are reaching another unique feature – the wonders of Objective-C runtime.

Let's see the following (and very short!) code:

```
class Album {

    var title : String
}
```

We obviously see the problem here – the Album class has no initializers.

But we can easily silence the compiler by adding the @NSManaged attribute:

```
class Album  {

    @NSManaged var title : String
}
```

The @NSManaged attribute tells the compiler, "Don't worry. I will implement the setter and getter of title during runtime."

What Core Data does with classes that are inherited from NSManagedObject is to dispatch setters and getters to properties that are marked with the @NSManaged attribute.

Dynamic dispatch is a unique feature of the Objective-C runtime that lets us dynamically dispatch method implementations.

What we need to do to help Core Data with that task is to create matched managed objects with identical names to our entities and identical property names to the entity's attributes:

```
class Album: NSManagedObject {

    @NSManaged var title: String
    @NSManaged var id: UUID
    @NSManaged var releaseDate: Date
}
```

And on our data model editor, it looks like this (Figure 3-4).

Figure 3-4. *Album entity on the data model editor*

Does this mean that we need to maintain a list of classes and be strict on the properties' naming?

Apparently, yes.

But doing that manually may not be the best way to handle that.

Fortunately, Xcode has a better solution for you (even more than one!).

Generated Classes

You didn't think we were going to spend most of our precious time maintaining Core Data classes, did you?

As I said earlier, Xcode has excellent solutions for you, and you can select your level of control.

The neat thing about choosing the control level is that you can select a different level of control for various entities.

Let's jump right into the process by going back to the data model editor and opening the Xcode inspector.

The Data Model Inspector

If you read this book, you are probably not new to how the Xcode user interface is built.

On the left side of the window, you can find the navigator to help you navigate through the different items from different types in your projects.

On the right part of the window, you can find the inspector pane used to customize the selected item, no matter where you are in your project.

The same goes for Core Data.

Select an entity in the Core Data editor and reveal the inspector.

To reveal the inspector, you can either choose from the menu View ➤ Inspectors ➤ Show Inspector, press Option+Command+0, or click the top-right button in the window.

Look at Figure 3-5.

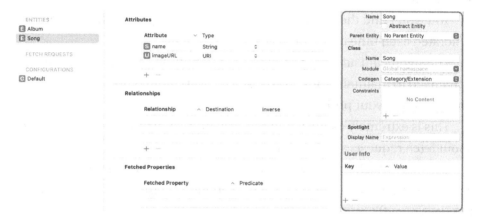

Figure 3-5. *The data model inspector*

Note   The data model inspector will be very useful for us going forward with this book.

In the data model inspector, you can find the "Codegen" popup menu. Clicking it opens three options – Manual/None, Class Definition, and Category/Extension.

Class Definition

Class Definition is the simplest and easiest way of generating managed classes for your Core Data entities.

What you need to do here is...nothing!

Yes, Class Definition is the "automatic" way of generating classes.

When you build your project, Xcode takes Core Data entities marked with Codegen Class Definition and generates classes with corresponding names and properties.

You won't find these classes on your project navigator – they are being generated each time and sent to your derived data.

The significant advantage of the Class Definition setting is that you don't need to maintain your classes at all – everything is done for you each time you build your project.

This is extremely useful when moving forward in our book and talking about fetch requests and relationships.

Let's see what happens when we try to right-click the expression and choose "Jump to Definition" on such a generated class in code (right-click the class name):

```
//
//  Song+CoreDataProperties.swift
//
//
//  Created by Avi Tsadok on 30/10/2021.
//
//  This file was automatically generated and should not
be edited.
//

import Foundation
import CoreData
```

```
extension Song {

    @nonobjc public class func fetchRequest() ->
    NSFetchRequest<Song> {
        return NSFetchRequest<Song>(entityName: "Song")
    }

    @NSManaged public var imageURL: URL?
    @NSManaged public var name: String?

}


extension Song : Identifiable {

}
```

You got to admit that may save you a lot of time.

But, as always, the big disadvantage of auto-generating code is its weakness. What if we want to customize "Song"? Add more methods or override setters and getters?

In other words, we want Xcode to generate classes, but we may also like the option to edit them.

Manual/None

When selecting the Manual/None option, Xcode does the opposite of Class Definition, meaning nothing.

Creating the classes is up to us, not Xcode.

One option, in this case, is to write the entities' classes ourselves. The other option is to generate them each time using Xcode.

To do that, we need to open our data model editor and select "Create NSManagedObject Subclass" from the editor menu.

Figures 3-6 and 3-7 show the two steps we need to do to select what entities we want to generate.

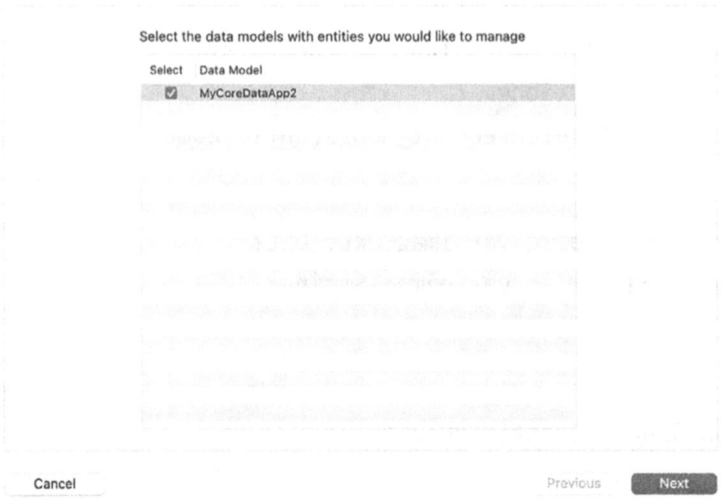

Select the data models with entities you would like to manage

Select	Data Model
☑	MyCoreDataApp2

Cancel   Previous   Next

Figure 3-6. *Select Data Model to generate*

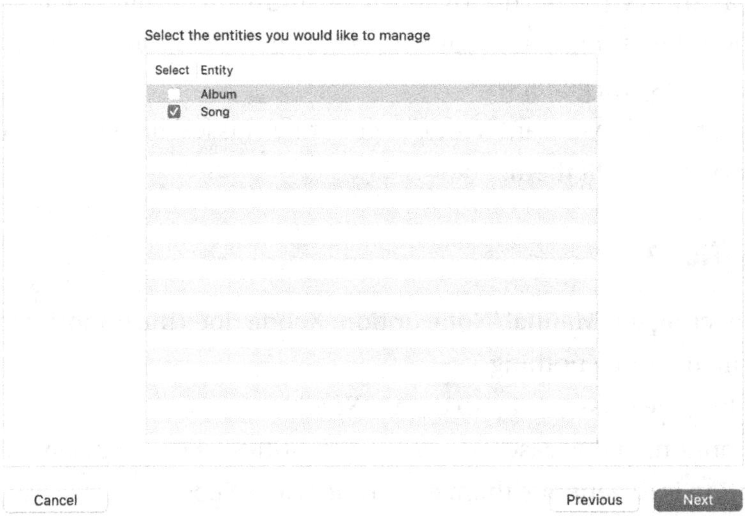

Select the entities you would like to manage

Select	Entity
☐	Album
☑	Song

Cancel   Previous   Next

Figure 3-7. *Select Entity to generate*

After we select a group and location to save the generated files, we get two files – Song+CoreDataClass and Song+CoreDataProperties.

If we open Song+CoreDataProperties, we'll see generated code similar to what we saw when we tried to inspect the same entity in Class Definition, but in this case, the file contains only an extension:

```
import Foundation
import CoreData

extension Song {

    @nonobjc public class func fetchRequest() ->
    NSFetchRequest<Song> {
        return NSFetchRequest<Song>(entityName: "Song")
    }

    @NSManaged public var imageURL: URL?
    @NSManaged public var name: String?
}

extension Song : Identifiable {

}
```

Looking at Song+CoreDataClass.swift reveals the class declaration itself:

```
import Foundation
import CoreData

@objc(Song)
public class Song: NSManagedObject {

}
```

The question is, Why did Xcode decide to create **two separate files** for each entity?

So that is something interesting Xcode is doing here.

A few years ago, Xcode generated one file and one file only for each entity.

Developers did two things: while adding and subclassing methods in the managed object class, they also added more attributes to the data model file.

For example, developers added code that responded to changes in the entity's data.

But when they regenerated the class using Xcode, they overwrote the files, and all the changes they did were gone.

Few third-party solutions solved the problem the same way Apple did at last – separate the class into two files: one that contains an extension with the properties and is being updated by the generator (Song+CoreDataProperties) and the other file for the developer to use (Song+CoreDataClass.swift).

Trying to regenerate the entity will overwrite **only** the properties extension, so you can safely change the class itself.

Category/Extension

If we stop for a moment and think hard, we may conclude that there can be another solution.

What if Xcode will keep maintaining the extension automatically with all the properties every time we change the data model and still, at the same time, the developer will maintain the class declaration?

It sounds like a mix of Manual and Class Definition, right? Right.

This is precisely what "Category/Extension" means. If you choose "Category/Extension," the properties extension will be created in the derived data and maintained by Xcode.

Xcode will generate the class declaration the same way it happens in "Manual/None."

Note Generating classes using "Category/Extension" may generate the class declaration in some Xcode versions. Not only it's a bug but it can also cause issues when trying to build the project due to an "invalid redeclaration" error. You can safely delete the extension file and keep the class declaration to solve that issue.

In some way, "Category/Extension" is the best of all worlds – maintaining properties for your attributes while giving you the flexibility you need to modify your classes.

Attributes Inspector

The data model inspector we discussed earlier is not relevant only for entities but also for their attributes.

Reveal the inspector like before, and tap on one of the attributes (Figure 3-8).

Figure 3-8. *The attributes inspector*

The inspector pane has four different inspectors – the first three inspect the file details, and the fourth, which is what we want to explore, inspects the selected item details.

The inspector structure can be different between the attributes. Some contain more configurations, according to their type.

Let's see what we can do to make our data configuration more flexible.

Optional

The Optional setting is a confusing one. Many developers think that Optional in Core Data is the same as Optional in Swift.

But when we set an attribute to be non-optional in Core Data and generate an NSManagedObject subclass file (as we learned before), the generated property will always be optional.

Optional in Core Data means that when we save the data, the optional property can be left empty (nil).

The reason Core Data generates an optional property, even if declared as non-optional, is the way Core Data works. When we create a new entity, the property is still empty, and until the time you need to save it, it's totally valid.

If Xcode generates a non-optional property for a non-optional attribute, any attempt to read it before the property is set will lead to a crash.

An excellent example of Optional usage is home phone numbers for contacts. The Optional point of view is from the data perspective and not Swift.

Transient

Transient attributes contain values that are not being saved in your persistent store (we'll talk about what "saved" means later).

They are usually being computed in real time, but they are still an integrated part of the Core Data model.

A classic example would be a "fullName" attribute:

```
var fullname : String {
    return (self.firstName ?? "") + " " + (self.
    lastName ?? "")
}
```

This can give you added "smart" properties without maintaining them.

Default Value

The "Default Value" setting is an important one. It lets set the default value of the entity's attribute when initializing the object.

Notice that the field is changed according to attribute type – for String attributes, the default value is just a text, but in numeric attributes, you can set a number, of course.

Now, put down the book and think for a moment about the relationship between the Optional setting and Default Value.

Can an attribute be optional and have a default value at the same time?

If you concluded that an attribute can be optional and have a default value at the same time, it means you understood how things work here. Good for you!

Those two settings are living in peace with each other.

Even if you set a default value for an attribute, it doesn't mean you cannot set it to nil.

Another thing you need to remember is that the default value is something that is set at the database level.

Generating an NSManagedObject subclass with a default value doesn't look like

```
@NSManaged public var title: String? = "Dark Side of The Moon"
```

The default value is relevant to newly created entities only.

Use Scalar Type

You already saw that Core Data attributes are generated as classes and not primitive types.

For example, the "Integer 16" type is represented as NSNumber and not int16 property.

What does it mean underneath? What happens precisely in the DB, in the case of the use of Sqlite3 or the binary store type?

So, for every attribute type, there's a scalar type – the type that is used in memory.

Going back to "Integer 16," we may see NSNumber in the generated managed object class, but its scalar type is indeed int16.

What about the other attribute types?

Let's look at Table 3-2.

Table 3-2. *Attribute Types and Their Scalar Types*

Attribute Type	Type	Scalar Type
Integer 16	NSNumber	Int16
Integer32	NSNumber	Int32
Integer 64	NSNumber	Int64
Double	NSNumber	Double
Float	NSNumber	Float
Boolean	NSNumber	Bool
Date	NSDate	TimeInterval
Decimal	NSDecimalNumber	NSDecimalNumber
UUID	UUID	UUID
URI	URL	-
String	String	-
Binary Data	Data	-
Transformable	NSObject	-

Table 3-2 shows the Core Data attribute types list and their scalar types, taken from the Apple Developer website (https://developer.apple.com/documentation/coredata/nsattributetype).

You've probably noticed that many types, especially numeric attribute types, are represented as NSNumber while they have primitive types underneath.

This may cause us quite a headache.

For starters, to use the actual type, we need to use NSNumber boolValue, doubleValue, int16Value, etc.

On the opposite direction, when setting a new value, we need to wrap it as NSNumber:

```
album.duration = NSNumber(value: 5.3)
```

What many developers did up until iOS 5 is to create getter and setter methods, to handle primitive types more comfortably.

While it may be a decent solution, there is a better one – the "Use Scalar Type" option.

Marking that option generates your classes with the primitive type for the properties instead of the value type.

Let's look at how the Float type looks when "Use Scalar Type" is enabled:

```
@NSManaged public var duration: Float // instead of NSNumber
```

One important thing to notice is that using scalar types doesn't affect Core Data's storage size.

Using scalar types should be according to your needs – for example, if you need the saved data for graphics calculations, using scalar types is ideal.

But if you need to add them to Obj-C NSArrays, wrapping them in NSNumber will be a hassle.

More Settings

It's true we have additional settings for attributes.

But Optional, Transient, Default Value, and Use Scalar Type are the basic settings you should know by now.

The other settings are related to other subjects and areas we will cover throughout the book.

Let's leave something for later!

Summary

We've talked about the Core Data model editor, what entities are and how to use them, how to add new entities and attributes, and how to configure them.

That was a lot for just entities! And there are plenty more to come!

But don't worry. In the next chapter, we'll talk about one of the most exciting features of Core Data – relationships!

CHAPTER 4

Relationships

Weeks of programming can save you hours of planning.

—Anonymous

In the previous chapter, we first discovered the data model and learned about entities.

But using Core Data for just managing entities is like buying a car for just sitting inside and hearing music – the sound may be excellent, but we are kind of missing the point here.

A significant part of the Core Data magic is connecting those entities and letting Core Data handle all the hard work.

In this chapter, we will learn

- Theoretical material about relationships and connections in databases

- How to configure relationships in Core Data using Xcode

- All about deletion rules and entity order

- Connecting entities in code

- How to build a tree or a graph data structure using relationships

© Avi Tsadok 2022
A. Tsadok, *Unleash Core Data*, https://doi.org/10.1007/978-1-4842-8211-3_4

Some Theory First

Before we dive into the relationship setup, let's talk about some theory first and discuss data schemes in general.

The primary three forms of linking between entities are basically

- One-to-many

- Many-to-many

- One-to-one

If you haven't heard of these three terms, let's straighten up before we continue.

One-to-Many

The one-to-many relationship is probably the most common one.

One-to-many states that an object from Entity A can be linked to multiple objects from Entity B, but every Entity B object can be linked to only one Entity A object.

To make things easier, think of a book with pages. Every "book" can have many "pages," but each "page" can only have one "book" (Figure 4-1).

Figure 4-1. *A Book-Page one-to-many relationship*

There are examples of one-to-many relationships from the real world – team and players, department and workers, or house and rooms.

What is usually common in one-to-many relationships is that we use it to **represent a hierarchy in our scheme**, and that could be your finger rule.

Many-to-Many

A many-to-many relationship is a more complex relationship than one-to-many.

In a many-to-many relationship, each object from Entity A can have many objects from Entity B. Still, each object from Entity B can also have many objects from Entity A.

Confused? Okay, here's an example – students and classes.

Each class can have multiple students, and each student can be registered to different classes (Figure 4-2).

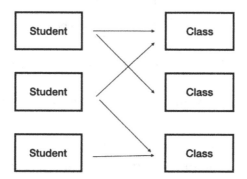

Figure 4-2. *Many-to-many relationship – students and classes*

The example of "Student" and "Class" is just a classic one. In general, a many-to-many relationship often represents a subscription or a registration between entities.

One-to-One

A one-to-one relationship is less common than one-to-many and many-to-many.

A one-to-one relationship means that every object of Entity A can have one and only one corresponding object of Entity B and vice versa.

A classic example is "Contact" and "Phone Number." Every "Contact" has only one "Phone Number," and each "Phone Number" belongs to one "Contact" only (Figure 4-3).

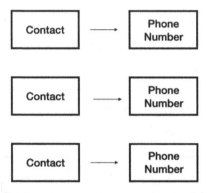

Figure 4-3. *One-to-one relationship, contacts and phone numbers*

Additional examples would be sales and receipts, car and chassis, or printer and tuner.

Just like one-to-many and many-to-many, if we want to find the finger rule here, one-to-one relationships represent an expansion of an entity data, just like the preceding examples.

Relationships in SQL Tables

To summarize things, the preceding three relationships are the basics of every data scheme you will build in Core Data (and not only!).

If we move forward to SQL, representation of these relationships in tables is being done using a primary key.

The primary key is the unique column that defines the row and identifies it in other tables.

Look at Figure 4-4.

Albums	
Id	title
1	Dark Side Of The Moon
2	Thriller

Songs		
Id	title	albumID
1	Speak to me	1
2	On the Run	1
3	Time	1
4	Beat It	2

Figure 4-4. *One-to-many relationship in SQL tables*

In Figure 4-4, we can see how one-to-many relationships are represented in SQL tables. We have an Albums table and a Songs table. Every album (and a song) has an ID, and in this case, the ID is the table's primary key.

To connect every song to its companion album, we have a particular column in the Songs table, called "albumID".

That way, we can also represent a one-to-one relationship and many-to-many relationship using an additional connecting table.

As you can see, there isn't any "built-in tool" to create relationships in SQL tables – it's up to us to maintain these relationships ourselves.

For example, deleting an album from the Albums table requires us to delete all its songs from the Songs table.

Everything is done using our primary key, and in more complex data schemes, things can become much more complicated.

It's easy to make mistakes, and when it happens, our database can become "corrupted" – entities such as book pages can float in our tables without being linked to a book.

So how are things done in Core Data?

Back to Xcode

Unlike SQL tables, relationships in Core Data are being handled by Core Data itself. Not only that entities in Core Data have a built-in "primary key" (which is not one of the attributes defined by you). Also, Core Data handles the ongoing maintenance of the relationship itself.

The way Core Data handles relationships is a huge advantage and a pretty good reason to use Core Data when handling complex data structures.

There are other great solutions for only maintaining entities, but "relationships" are where Core Data really shines.

Creating Our First Relationship

Unlike relationships in real life, setting up a new one is very simple when using Core Data. Let's open Xcode in the data model editor and look at the "Relationships" section under the Attributes section (Figure 4-5).

Figure 4-5. *Relationships section*

The Relationships section displays all the relationships the specific entity has with the other entities.

The Relationships table has three columns – Relationship, Destination, and Inverse.

For the sake of an example, we will continue using the fun example of music – albums and songs.

- **Relationship (name)** or just **Relationship** contains the name of the relationship **from the point of view of this entity**. For example, if the current entity is an album, and we want to represent its songs, we might name it "songs". The name of the relationship should be declarative and clear.

- The **Destination** is the other entity our relationship is linked to. In this case, if the current entity is Album, the destination should be "Song".

- This is a relationship from Album to Song. In the Song entity, we should have another relationship from Song to Album. The **Inverse** is the returned relationship that Song has back to Album.

The Inverse part is essential. When we link two entities (A and B) together, we need to create two relationships – from A to B and B to A. In fact, a relationship in Core Data is one way only. So, to actually link two entities, we need to define how to approach each other from both ways.

Let's see this line closely after filling up the details (Figure 4-6).

∨ **Relationships**

Relationship	∧ Destination	Inverse
🅞 songs	Song	⌃ album ⌃

Figure 4-6. *Album-to-Song relationship*

If you follow my steps, the Inverse should still be empty. That's okay; we haven't yet created the relationship from Song to Album. We'll do it soon.

Looking closely at Figure 4-6, you can see a red square and an "O" right in its center. This means that the relationship to Song is "to-one."

If we go back to the theory part at the beginning of the chapter, "to-one" means that for each album, we have one, and only one, song.

This is definitely not what we want in the case of albums and songs.

But don't worry! We can change that easily using the data model inspector.

Configure Our Relationship

Just like entities and attributes, relationships also have their own data model inspector on the right pane.

Tapping on the relationship reveals the inspector (Figure 4-7).

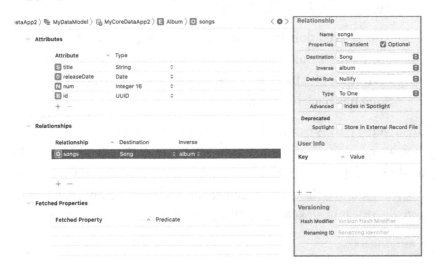

Figure 4-7. *Configuring the relationship using the inspector*

Some of the settings you see in the inspector were already discussed earlier – Name, Destination, and Inverse. But we can see there are additional interesting settings that power up relationships.

Relationship Type

The first and probably the most important one is **Type**.

There are two options – "To One" and "To Many."

Remember, because relationships in Core Data are one way only, we need to provide two relationships to connect two entities, one from each side.

Now that we know that relationships are one way only, we can understand why the options are only "To One" and "To Many." Using these two options can help us create all the relationship combinations we discussed earlier in this book.

Notice that changing the relationship type also changes the little icon next to the relationship name in the relationships list (Figure 4-8).

Figure 4-8. *Relationship type icon*

Delete Rule

Delete Rule for a relationship is a **critical part** you need to know before setting up your data scheme.

Delete Rule is another part of Core Data that magically represents your most profound and most important business principles.

"Delete Rule" answers the question, What happens to the destination object when you (try to) delete the current entity?

And this is a fundamental question. Going back to our Album-Song example, we can think of possible interesting thoughts:

- What happens if an album is deleted? Do we delete all its songs?

- And if it's a playlist, do we still delete its songs?

- If we want to allow deletion only for empty albums/ playlists, can we do it?

- What if we want to go wild and allow deletion only for albums that have less than five songs?

The preceding questions are only a fraction of our project core logic.

Now, in a pre–Core Data world, we usually manually implement the answers to those questions in our code.

For example, if an album deletion means deleting all its songs, we would need to go and delete its songs manually.

And if deleting a song means deleting additional entities, that's something we should also address ourselves.

What is exciting about Core Data is that we get (some of) the deletion logic for free!

Back to the data model editor, we have four different deletion rules – No Action, Nullify, Cascade, and Deny.

Nullify

We'll start with the Nullify rule.

If, in my preface for deletion rules, I described complicated questions and logic, the "Nullify" rule states for just "do nothing."

Yes, there are many cases where we just want to delete an entity without any side effects whatsoever.

In our (already became classic) example of songs and albums, if we delete a song, we **don't** want to delete its album.

A many-to-one relationship is a classic example of using Nullify. A less classic example is one-to-one.

In this case, when we delete an entity with the Nullify rule, it just sets its relationship to nil – just cutting it.

The same goes for a one-to-many relationship. If we delete an album, setting the relationship deletion rule to Nullify may leave its songs without an album.

If we do need side effects for our deletion, the Cascade rule is a better fit.

Cascade

The Cascade rule is much more "dramatic" than Nullify. The Cascade rule says, "Deleting the source entity will also delete the destination entity."

Now, Cascade is a very powerful rule, so we should use it carefully. When we think of it, Cascade is the only rule that may start a recursive deletion action because of its side effects.

Let's look at the example in Figure 4-9.

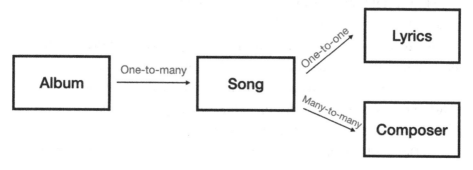

Figure 4-9. *Cascade deletion rule side effects*

Let's imagine what happens if all the three relationships in the diagram have the Cascade deletion rule.

Deleting an album would delete all its songs. That's good.

As a result, all the songs' lyrics will be deleted as well. That also sounds like a logical behavior.

Another side effect is that Core Data will also delete all the songs' composers.

Because composers have additional songs in different albums, deleting them due to an album removal is the kind of side effect we don't want in our data model.

In the case of the relationship to the composer, the deletion rule should be, of course, Nullify.

As you can see, the Cascade rule is powerful and can lead to unwanted results if not taken carefully.

Deny

Here is another powerful deletion rule we can use. Deny is precisely the opposite of Cascade.

Now, pay attention carefully, as this part may be a little confusing.

When setting a Deny deletion rule from A to B, Core Data will refuse to delete Entity A if there are any entities B linked to it.

Let's describe that again with Album and Song.

If the relationship between Album and Song has a **Cascade** rule, it means that all its songs will be deleted whenever we delete an album.

If the relationship between Album and Song has a **Deny** rule, it means that whenever we delete an album, if there are any songs linked to this album, Core Data will reject the removal action.

The Deny rule's goal is to protect our data from being **corrupted** by having orphan entities in our store "without a parent."

When setting up relationships, we need to conclude our business logic inside, and the thumb rules I just gave can help you with that.

We can even have custom deletion logic, but we will touch it later in the book.

Arrangement (Only for "To-Many" Relationships)

Like many other things in life, we always need to understand our needs and conclude the costs.

When we have a "to-many" relationship, the destination object is actually a collection of objects.

The objects collection can be ordered or non-ordered.

In code, eventually, it will be represented as NSSet vs. NSOrderedSet.

Without getting into many details, NSSet is much faster than NSOrderedSet in most operations. Still, things may become a little bit different when we constantly need the items to be ordered.

Now, there are other ways for the collection to be ordered.

We can use one of the attributes to do that – sorting the objects by date or by a number is a good example.

Putting performance aside for a second, it is not a best practice to let a (any) data store handle your data ordering.

The reason is that data ordering is usually done according to some logic. It can be derived from the time we inserted the object (then we can use a Date attribute) or dynamically ordered by size (Int) or update time (again, Date).

Leave Core Data to deal with other stuff for you and handle the ordering yourself.

Count (Again, Only for "To-Many" Relationships)

Another feature a "to-many" relationship has for us is the option to limit the number of entities in our destination collection (see Figure 4-10).

Figure 4-10. *Count limitation for a relationship*

We can set the minimum and maximum number of entities in the collection, and if the collection holds a different count, saving the changes will eventually fail.

We'll discuss validation later in the book, but adding constraints to our Core Data is a good idea as long as we know how to handle our business logic and UI layer errors.

Let's Take a Breath

If you feel a little bit overwhelmed by what we've learned till now about relationships in Core Data, that's fine.

Data schemes are naturally complex because the data itself is sometimes complex.

Remember, our data architecture is the heart and soul of our app. The more complex your app gets, the more complex the data scheme will be.

Core Data is here to make things simpler, cleaner, and organized.

Before we continue, I suggest making sure you understand this part and reread the material again if needed.

Editor Style

We haven't talked about the design of the data model editor screen. It's not that there isn't anything interesting there – I just want to show you that later in the book.

One neat feature of the data model editor when speaking about relationships between entities is the Editor Style.

If you look at the right bottom corner, you'll see a button with two modes called "Editor Style" (Figure 4-11).

Figure 4-11. *Editor Style button in the data model editor*

Those of you who used Microsoft Access in the past surely remember when you could visually look at your tables and see their connections to each other.

Well, Xcode has this feature as well. The "Editor Style" button has two modes – "Table" and "Graph." And up until now, we used the "Table" mode for our work.

Switching to the "Graph" mode reveals a totally new layout of our entities while displaying the connections in a visual way (Figure 4-12).

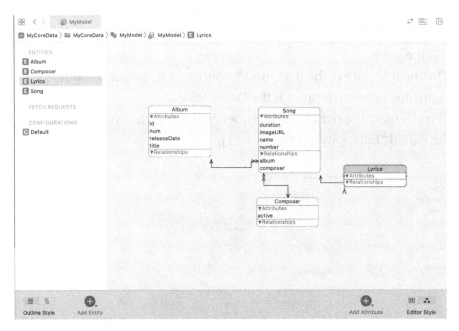

Figure 4-12. *Data model editor, style "Graph"*

Think of the new style as your "Storyboard for Data" feature.

The "Graph" mode is constructive when you work on your app and try to keep your entity relationships logical by seeing all of them in one place.

I must say that when your app grows and your data becomes much more complex, it is much harder to use this feature, as the screen gets loaded with entities and relationships.

Using it at an early stage of your app can be very useful.

Let's Return to Code

When we've learned about attributes, we talked about
NSEntitiyDescription, which holds the entity's definition.

As part of the definition, we can retrieve the entity's attribute list by
accessing the variable attributesByName():

```
let songEntityDescription = delegate.persistentContainer.
managedObjectModel.entitiesByName["Song"]
```

```
let titleAttributeDescription = songEntityDescription.
attributesByName["title"]
```

titleAttributeDescription has all the information for the title
attribute we defined in our data model.

The same goes for relationships. We can retrieve all our relationships
from the description using the variable relationshipsByName.

For example, to get the relationship between "Song" and "Composer,"
we need to write

```
let songEntityDescription = delegate.persistentContainer.
managedObjectModel.entitiesByName["Song"]
```

```
let toComposer = songEntityDescription.relationshipsByName
["composer"]
```

toComposer is an instance of NSRelationshipDescription and has all
the information we discussed earlier.

When we discussed the dynamic nature of the data model, we said we
could build our whole data model with code – NSRelationshipDescription
helps us set up the relationships programmatically.

Connecting Entities Together

Remember we are not here for only theoretical material.

How do we actually use the fantastic relationships we've just learned how to build?

The first approach is to use the NSManagedObject key/value technique, the same way we did when we set our attributes:

```
let song = NSEntityDescription.insertNewObject(forEntityName: "Song", into: context)

let composer = NSEntityDescription.insertNewObject(forEntityName: "Composer", into: context)

song.setValue(composer, forKey: "composer")
```

In the preceding code, we create a new "Song" and a new "Composer" and then set the composer to the new song, using a simple setValue method.

The key "composer" is the name of the relationship we defined earlier.

Now it's time for you to scratch your head and think, "But we can automatically generate the NSManagedObject subclass for attributes. Can't we do the same for relationships?"

The answer is that we can!

Let's look at the class Song, which Xcode generated:

```
@NSManaged public var duration: Float
@NSManaged public var imageURL: URL?
@NSManaged public var name: String?
@NSManaged public var number: Int32
@NSManaged public var album: Album?
@NSManaged public var composer: Composer?
@NSManaged public var lyrics: Lyrics?
@NSManaged public var playlists: NSSet?
```

```
}
```

```
// MARK: Generated accessors for playlists
extension Song {

    @objc(addPlaylistsObject:)
    @NSManaged public func addToPlaylists(_ value: Playlist)

    @objc(removePlaylistsObject:)
    @NSManaged public func removeFromPlaylists(_ value:
    Playlist)

    @objc(addPlaylists:)
    @NSManaged public func addToPlaylists(_ values: NSSet)

    @objc(removePlaylists:)
    @NSManaged public func removeFromPlaylists(_ values: NSSet)

}
```

Do you see how much work Xcode has done for us?

To understand the changes, we need to distinguish between to-one and to-many relationships.

When it's a "to-one" relationship, there's a property with the relationship's name and the type of the destination:

```
 @NSManaged public var lyrics: Lyrics?
```

When it's a "to-many" relationship, we also have a property:

```
@NSManaged public var playlists: NSSet?
```

We see that the property's type is no longer the destination's type, which is NSSet.

If you recall, earlier, we talked about the "arrangement" of entities in a "to-many" relationship, and we had a checkbox saying whether it should be ordered or not.

A non-ordered relationship will be generated as NSSet and an ordered one as NSOrderedSet.

Another exciting thing Xcode has generated for us is helper methods to add and remove Playlist objects.

There are two sets of methods – the first for adding and removing a single object and the second for adding and removing a collection of elements (a set as well).

Now, let's continue with a series of interesting questions:

- If we remove objects in a "to-many" relationship using a dedicated "remove" method, how do we remove a "to-one" relationship?

- We know that a "one-to-many" relationship is actually two Core Data relationships – one side is "to-one," and the other side is "to-many." What is the right way to unlink the connection?

- What does it mean about the deletion rule we discussed earlier?

True, removing a "to-many" relationship is done using a remove method.

For a "to-one" relationship, it's even simpler – we just **set the generated property to nil**.

The fun part is that when we deal with a "one-to-many" relationship, setting nil in the "to-one" relationship is precisely like removing the object in the "to-many" relationship side.

Both ways regarding the deletion rule, removing an object and setting it to nil, activate the deletion rule. The deletion rule is something that is enforced when we save our changes to the context, so don't worry about it.

A Relationship to Itself

Can we create a relationship between Entity A and...the same Entity A?

The answer is yes!

We can point entities to each other the same as other relationships, and it is perfectly fine and legit!

Look at Figure 4-13.

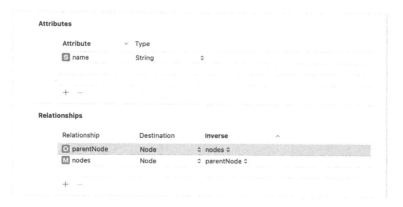

Figure 4-13. *Relationship to "self"*

Figure 4-13 displays a way to create a tree structure using two relationships:

- A "to-many" relationship to children nodes

- An inverse "to-one" relationship to the parent node

If we change the "to-one" relationship to "to-many," we can even create a whole graph.

Let's see how the Node entity looks in the data model editor when we change to the graph view (Figure 4-14).

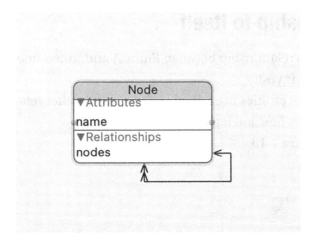

Figure 4-14. *Node tree in the data model editor graph view*

Now, take a moment – can you think about the deletion rule in this case?

Summary

We just covered an essential aspect of Core Data and one of its main advantages.

Now it's time to move forward with our Core Data stack and connect our entities to our app using context.

CHAPTER 5

Contexts

Good programmers know what's beautiful and bad ones don't.

—D. Gelernter (*Machine Beauty*, Basic Books, 1998)

Until now, we've discussed how to set up our Core Data stack and define our entities and their relationships, but we really haven't talked about **working with these entities**.

When I say "working," I mean creating entities and fetching, updating, or deleting them.

Well, now we have reached the money time!

In this chapter, we will learn

- What are contexts

- How to insert, fetch, and delete objects

- How to predefine fetch requests in our data model editor

- How to work with multiple contexts

Ready? Let's jump in.

© Avi Tsadok 2022
A. Tsadok, *Unleash Core Data*, https://doi.org/10.1007/978-1-4842-8211-3_5

What Are Contexts?

Contexts are the top layer of our Core Data stack. They connect our code to the persistent store and the data model, and we use them to manipulate and modify our objects.

Working with objects is always according to a specific context – because context is not just the object that fetches data but also the object that tracks data changes.

In general, contexts have several goals:

- Creating new objects

- Fetching objects

- Tracking changes

- Validation

- Handling undo/redo

- Isolating data modifications from our persistent store

The preceding goals list length is an excellent indication of how much central contexts are in Core Data programming. Most of your daily work will be dealing with contexts rather than handling the other levels of the stack.

But what are contexts **exactly**?

The Concept

I've mentioned before that sometimes, to assimilate a new concept, we should approach it as we are those who plan it.

Let's do some guided imagery together.

We have a persistent store, fetching data and representing them as instances. Now, at this point, several things can happen. For example, our data store can change, and at the same time, our fetched objects can be modified by the user.

That (not uncommon) situation brings up interesting questions and conflicts we need to solve. For example, how to deal with data being changed in one place while we are trying to fetch and display it in another place?

So what we want to do is to disconnect what we're doing in our fetched objects from what is happening in other places in our app.

This is kind of what contexts in Core Data are doing. They let us "play" with our data, isolated from the rest of the stack.

Scratch Pad

Contexts are a **scratch pad** for our data.

More terms I can use here are maybe a "playground" or a "sandbox," but you get the idea.

To "commit" changes, we need to call the context's save() method. What happens then?

That's a good question.

Let's leave that for later and start manipulating some data.

Creating a Context

So how do we create a context?

You'll be glad to know that contexts are like Apple's warranty – you get the first year for free.

Looking at our persistent container object, we'll see a property named viewContext of type NSManagedObjectContext.

That will be our main context to be used on the main thread.

To create another context, we can initialize it this way:

```
let newContext = NSManagedObjectContext(concurrencyType:
.mainQueueConcurrencyType)
```

To create a context to be used on a private thread, we can just pass `privateQueueConcurrencyType` as the `concurrencyType` or create a new background context:

```
let privateContext = persistentContainer.newBackgroundContext()
```

Private context is used to work with data on a background thread.

Every Core Data object belongs to one context and has a `managedObjectContext` property that points to its context.

Manipulating Data

We need to know a couple of basic actions to start using Core Data contexts effectively, such as **insert**, **delete**, or **fetch**.

If you are used to SQL, you will notice some differences here.

Don't worry – we need to get used to a different state of mind.

Insert New Objects

The first thing I want to show you is how to **create new objects**. Now, it's very important not to be confused here, so I'll remind you some of the terms we've learned till now:

Entity – Type of object. Equivalent to "class" in object-oriented programming or "table" in SQL

Entity Description – The declaration of the entity

Based on that, if we want to create a new record, we don't "insert a new entity," but we instantiate an existing entity.

We have two ways to create a Core Data object:

```
// first way
let newObject = NSEntityDescription.
insertNewObject(forEntityName: "Song", into: context)
```

```
// second way
let songEntityDescription = appDelegate.persistentContainer.
managedObjectModel.entitiesByName["Song"]!
let newObject = NSManagedObject(entity: songEntityDescription,
insertInto: context)
```

Both ways practically do the same, but with a different approach. The first way is the more popular and also shorter. We use a static method of NSEntityDescription and insert an object by its name.

The second way first loads an entity directly from the data model and afterward initializes an NSManagedObject with the entity we just loaded.

Notice that we use our context in both ways and pass it to the object we've just created.

As I said, we'll use the first and shorter way to create objects in most cases. We have the second way as well because we have multiple stores or when we want to create an entity description manually in code.

Now that we have an NSManagedObject, we probably want to cast it to the subclass we generated from our data model:

```
let song = newObject as? Song
```

Casting newObject to Song (in this case, of course) is essential if we want to use the attributes and methods Core Data generated for us.

```
song.title = "The Great Gig in the Sky"
```

To save the new record, we need to call the context's save() method:

```
try context.save()
```

As I said earlier, we'll talk about what exactly "save a context" means. Now let's talk about fetching objects from our store.

Fetching Objects

Fetching objects is easier than you think.

The primary thing to understand is that fetching objects from Core Data is based on something called a "fetch request."

A fetch request is an instance that holds all the fetching criteria for a fetching action.

Think of it as an enhanced and sophisticated data query.

Let's see a fetch request in action:

```
let fetchRequest = NSFetchRequest<Song>(entityName: "Song")
let songs = try context.fetch(fetchRequest)
```

The preceding two lines represent the basics of fetching objects in Core Data.

In this example, we are fetching **all the songs** in our store. Notice that the component that is doing the fetching itself is the context and not the fetch request.

To create a fetch request, we have several options.

The first option is to initialize it as the preceding example while passing the entity's name we want to fetch as a string:

```
let fetchRequest = NSFetchRequest<Song>(entityName: "Song")
```

We need to pass the result type as a generic value to the fetch request.

If we don't have an NSManagedObject subclass, we can pass NSFetchRequestResult and cast the result later:

```
let fetchRequest = NSFetchRequest<NSFetchRequestResult>
(entityName: "Song")
```

fetchRequest() Method

If we do have an NSManagedObject subclass, we have an even easier way:

```
let fetchRequest = Song.fetchRequest()
```

If you'll go back to the Chapter 3 where I explained about the entity class auto-generated, you will notice Xcode also generated a public class method called fetchRequest():

```
@nonobjc public class func fetchRequest() ->
NSFetchRequest<Song> {
        return NSFetchRequest<Song>(entityName: "Song")
}
```

Xcode does it because passing the entity name as a string may cause code safety issues such as typos and outdated entity names, so you are more than welcome to use it.

Add a Predicate

While the use of fetch requests is simple, it might be "too simple" for us. Currently, without any modifications, the fetch request returns **all the instances** from the provided entity.

It's only natural that we would like to filter it somehow.

Fortunately, a fetch request supports adding an NSPredicate.

You might know NSPredicate from other frameworks in iOS development.

For example, we use predicates for filtering NSArrays (Not Array – NSArray), calendar events, or contacts.

In Core Data fetch requests, NSPredicate is similar, even though it has some minor differences we'll discuss in detail later in the book.

To add a predicate to the fetch request, we just need to set its optional predicate property.

For example, the following code snippet filters Songs by their name:

```
let fetchRequest = Song.fetchRequest()
let predicate = NSPredicate(format: "name = %@", "Time")
fetchRequest.predicate = predicate
```

If the predicate is not valid, for example, the attributes are misspelled or the whole format is invalid, we'll get an exception when trying to fetch results from the context.

Sorting

When fetching objects from Core Data using NSFetchRequest, they will be returned randomly.

One option is to sort them **after** receiving them, but we lose the optimizations Core Data provides us.

NSFetchRequest has a property named sortDescriptors.

NSSortDescriptor is an object that describes how to sort data according to a key and sort order.

Here's an example of a sort descriptor by creation date, in an ascending order:

```
let dateSortDescriptor = NSSortDescriptor(key: "creationDate",
ascending: true)
```

To add the descriptor to our fetch request, we add it to our "sort descriptors" array:

```
songsFetchRequest.sortDescriptors = [dateSortDescriptor]
```

The reason sortDescriptors is an array is that NSFetchRequest has an additional neat feature – we can provide multiple sort descriptors and prioritize them.

For example, if we want to sort songs by creation date and, if the creation date is equal, then sort by name, we can provide two sort descriptors:

```
let dateSortDescriptor = NSSortDescriptor(key: "creationDate",
ascending: true)
let nameSortDescriptor = NSSortDescriptor(key: "name",
ascending: true)
```

```
songsFetchRequest.sortDescriptors = [dateSortDescriptor,
nameSortDescriptor]
```

Note   If you feel confused between sorting and ordered items
in a relationship, that's fine. Remember, we are talking about two
different things here – one is how objects are ordered in a to-many
relationship, and the second is related to NSFetchRequest only.

Fetch Offset and Limit

NSFetchRequest also has an interesting integer property named
fetchOffset:

```
request.fetchOffset = 10
```

What fetchOffset does is to return results from a specific "row index."
For example, a request without an offset returns the following objects:

> [a, b, c, d, e, f, g, h]

A request with an offset of 3 will skip the first three items and start from
object "d":

> [d, e, f, g, h]

fetchOffset goes great together with another property named
fetchLimit, which, as its name suggests, limits the results you receive.

Now, take a second and think of great usage for combining those two
properties.

Do you have something in mind?

Well, one significant usage will be implementing infinity scroll in
table views.

Fetching each time a small amount of data and moving the offset forward with each request can be beneficial on big data sets.

Considering Context Changes

Earlier, we said that contexts are like scratch pads. At first, they reflect what we have in our store, then we can modify them (add or manipulate objects), and the changes are being pushed only after we save them.

What does it mean for fetch requests? Do fetch requests include unsaved changes?

The answer is yes, but we can change that easily.

NSFetchRequest has a Boolean property named includePendingChanges, with a default value of true.

If we want to exclude unsaved changes, we need to set the property value to false.

Fetch Objects by ID

Core Data gives us the feeling that we are entering a non-ID world.

This is partially true – we usually add an ID to objects when we need to synchronize them with some backend service.

But regardless of any custom ID we may add to our entities, every Core Data object has its own internal ID that helps us identify it in our data store.

Core Data saves that ID in a property named objectID.

The objectID property is not a String or an Int – it is a value from a class named NSManagedObjectID.

Now, the objectID property is usually used to locate the same object between different contexts, which is a subject that we'll cover in a few pages.

If you have an objectID, you can fetch its object using the context's existingObject method:

```
let newSong = try context.existingObject(with: objectID)
```

Remember that objectID is the "real" object identifier when dealing with Core Data records.

Delete Objects

Deleting an object is one of the most straightforward actions for contexts.

Once we have the NSManagedObject in memory, all we need to do is call the delete() method:

```
context.delete(song)
```

Do you see? It is very simple. Nevertheless, the real complexity lies underneath.

If you remember the deletion rules from the previous chapter and the chain action they may start, you won't look at this operation as "simple."

Analyze what it means to delete an object, and consider carefully all the side effects it may cause.

Predefined Fetch Requests

You already understood that fetch requests are highly sophisticated – they contain great features and are very easy to use.

When we created entities, I first showed you how to create them in the data model editor and how to do the same in code.

With fetch requests, I showed you how to create them in code, but did you know that the data model editor gives you the ability to predefine them just like entities?

Let's go back to the data model editor. Look at Figure 5-1.

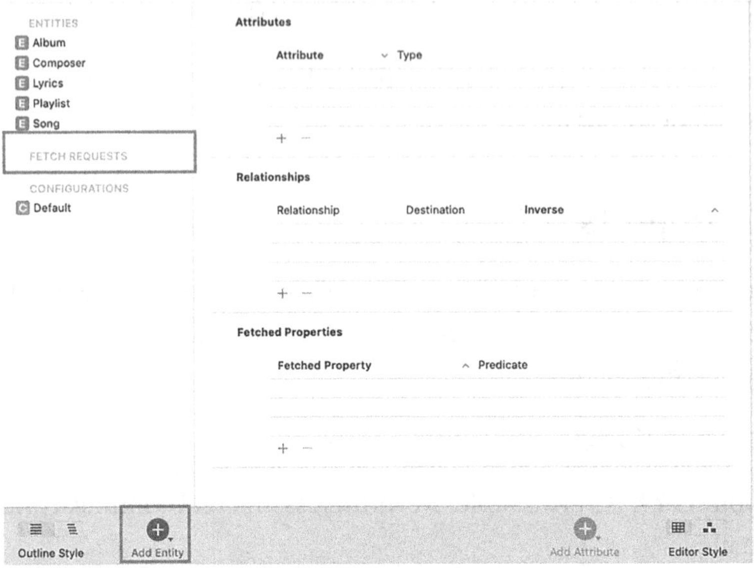

Figure 5-1. *Data model fetch requests*

Under the Entities list, you can see a section called "Fetch Requests."

As part of the data model, you can predefine fetch requests instead of creating them in code.

To create a new fetch request, click "Add Entity" at the bottom (marked in Figure 5-1 as well) and select "Add Fetch Request."

After your selection, a new fetch request will appear in the Fetch Requests list (Figure 5-2).

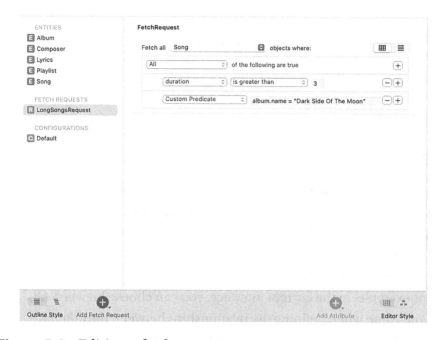

Figure 5-2. *Editing a fetch request*

Tapping on the new fetch request reveals an interface that can help you create a fetch request while combining multiple predicates easily and intuitively.

In this interface, we can

- Select what entity we want to fetch.

- Choose the condition type (All/Any/ None).

- Add predicates as many as we want.

The interface is straightforward; still, there are some interesting features you should know.

First, we can add custom predicates. That option doesn't tie us to the "regular" predicates Xcode offers us and provides us great flexibility.

Second, look at Figure 5-3.

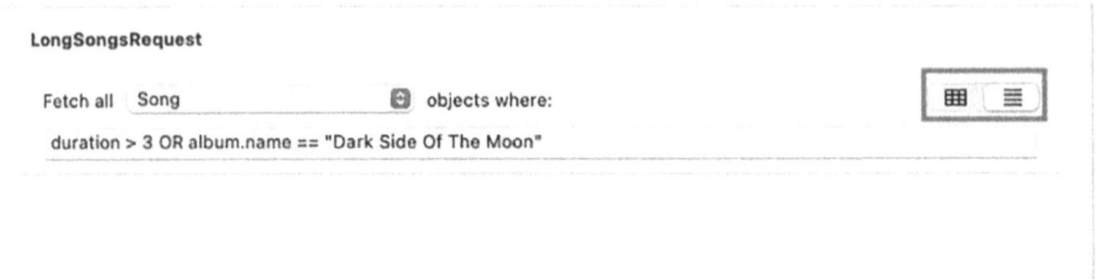

LongSongsRequest

Fetch all   Song   ⊕ objects where: ⊞ ≡

duration > 3 OR album.name == "Dark Side Of The Moon"

Figure 5-3. *Fetch request view mode*

In Figure 5-3, we have a button that switches between two views. Click it to change the fetch request predicates to one long predicate we can modify or use in our code.

Modifying the written predicate that we see opens new possibilities to create more sophisticated predicates.

For example, in the current interface, you can choose between All, Any, and None when defining the relationships between the different predicates.

If we choose "All" and switch to code view, we can see Xcode attaches the different statements with the "AND" operator between them.

If we change one of them to "OR" and then go back to the previous view, we can see we created a new section (Figure 5-4).

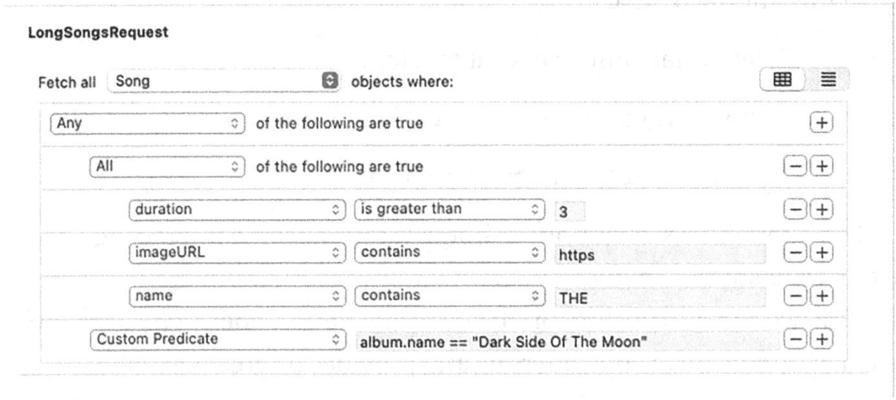

LongSongsRequest

Fetch all   Song   ⊕ objects where: ⊞ ≡

Any   ⌄ of the following are true   ⊕

All   ⌄ of the following are true   ⊖ ⊕

duration   ⌄ is greater than   ⌄ 3   ⊖ ⊕

imageURL   ⌄ contains   ⌄ https   ⊖ ⊕

name   ⌄ contains   ⌄ THE   ⊖ ⊕

Custom Predicate   ⌄ album.name == "Dark Side Of The Moon"   ⊖ ⊕

Figure 5-4. *Creating a new statement section*

100

More Predefined Fetch Request Configurations

If you recall, when we created fetch requests in our code, we had additional properties we could change.

For example, we could set the batch size or change the limit.

Well, we can do the same here.

Just like any other entity in Xcode, we need to open the inspector pane while the fetch request is selected (Figure 5-5).

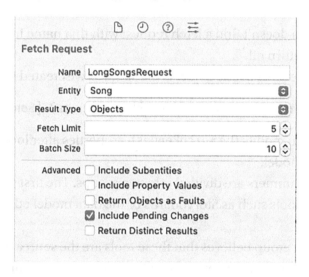

Figure 5-5. *Changing fetch request settings*

Note   There are additional properties we haven't covered yet. Don't worry. We'll get to them later.

Use Predefined Fetch Requests

We need to remember that we created them in our data model to use predefined fetch requests.

Therefore, when we load them in our code, we do that using our data model:

```
let fetchRequest = persistentContainer.managedObjectModel.
fetchRequestTemplate(forName: "LongSongsRequest")
```

If Core Data doesn't find a fetch request with that name in our data model, it will return nil.

Using the fetchRequest object is the same as we created it in code:

```
let songs = try context.fetch(fetchRequest) as? [Song]
```

We can even modify the fetchRequest properties after loading them from the data model.

Most programmers are divided into two groups. The first group likes to use built-in tools such as Storyboards or the data model editor to build their projects.

The second group believes that these tools are the source of all evil in the world and we should all build everything in code and code only.

Without getting into that argument, building predefined fetch requests has one big advantage.

When we work on big projects with many entities and attributes, it is very easy to get into typo mistakes, especially when we often change our data model.

Creating predefined fetch requests in the data model ensures that the fetch requests are already up to date with the changes we make in our projects.

Note   Another way to ensure we don't break our code when making changes is, of course, unit tests. Core Data fully supports unit tests, so just use them.

Multiple Contexts

At the beginning of the chapter, I told you I would tell you precisely what the save() method does.

Well, now is the time!

When we call save(), in most cases, we are pushing the changes back into our persistent store (as you probably guessed).

Now, there are reasons we call a context a "scratch pad," and the changes are being pushed only on save().

The main reason is that manipulating data in a living app can be complex and challenging.

Therefore, there are cases where we need multiple "scratch pads," or in our case multiple contexts.

Let's describe some of the cases:

- We sync our data with a backend service while we don't want to interrupt our app flow.

- We have several windows (on a Mac or iPad app), and the user can edit the same document in several places.

- The user enters an editor mode when they can abort their editing and go back to the main screen.

Now, that was just the tip of the ice. Projects today are sophisticated and, as a result, require sophisticated solutions.

Let's start with talking about multiple-main context apps.

Multiple Main Contexts

When we first talked about contexts, I said that you get the first one for free and that you can create additional contexts and connect them to the same store.

Holding two main contexts might cause conflicts in data when the same value is being modified from different directions.

The default approach for Core Data in that situation is **Optimistic Locking**.

Optimistic Locking

Once again, a context is like a playground. It's a sandbox that is isolated from the store, and without calling the save() method, changes stay within the context.

Now, think of a situation where we need to manage two playgrounds, for example, when the user edits two documents at the same time.

Let's describe a scenario:

–   The user opens document A under context a.

–   The user opens document B under context b.

–   The user modifies an entity in document A and saves it.

–   The user modifies the same entity in document B and saves it.

Look at Figure 5-6.

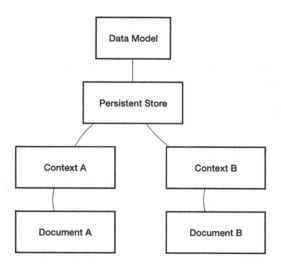

Figure 5-6. *Multiple main contexts*

With the preceding scenario, the user tries **to edit the same entity** in two different places simultaneously.

Now let's see how Core Data handles that situation underneath.

When we fetch an object from a context, Core Data takes a snapshot of the object data from the persistent store, including its to-one relationship.

When the user saves the object back, Core Data compares the snapshot to the current object data in the persistent store to see if anything has changed since the object was initially fetched.

If the snapshot and the object's current persistent data are equal, it's all great, and the context will be saved successfully.

If the object's current persistent state is different from the snapshot taken, it means that the object was changed during the editing, and Core Data will abort the save action.

This approach is called **Optimistic Locking**.

Optimistic Locking assumes that while the user edits an object, the persistent data it was based on hasn't been changed for the same values that were edited by the user.

The action where we need to push the context changes to the persistent store is called "merge."

Core Data causes the merge action to fail because that's the default merge policy, and we've got two options to handle these kinds of situations: change the policy or take that ourselves.

Merge Conflict Errors

Before touching the merge policy, let's see how the conflict looks in code.

Let's look at a code snippet where we try to update the same value in the same object in two different contexts:

```
let context = delegate.persistentContainer.viewContext

let context2 = NSManagedObjectContext(concurrencyType:
.mainQueueConcurrencyType)

context2.persistentStoreCoordinator = delegate.
persistentContainer.persistentStoreCoordinator

let predicate = NSPredicate(format: "name = %@", "Speak to me")
let fetchRequest = NSFetchRequest<Song>(entityName: "Song")
fetchRequest.predicate = predicate

   do {
              let songFromContext1 = try context.
              fetch(fetchRequest).first!
              let songFromContext2 = try context2.
              fetch(fetchRequest).first!
              songFromContext1.duration = 60.0
              songFromContext2.duration = 40.0

              try context.save()
              try context2.save()
```

```
} catch let error {
    NSLog((error as NSError).userInfo.debugDescription)
}
```

In the preceding code, we

- Created two contexts

- Connected them to the same persistent store

- Created a fetch request

- Loaded the same song from the two contexts

- Changed the duration on both instances

- Tried to save both entities

- Printed the received error

Now, you probably saw the conflict here.

But what's more interesting here is that I cast the Error object to NSError, which contains a userInfo dictionary of its own.

The NSError userInfo contains helpful information to understand precisely why our saving operation has failed. Let's look at the printed information:

```
["NSExceptionOmitCallstacks": 1, "conflictList": <__NSArrayM
0x600002850db0>(
NSMergeConflict (0x600003356800) for NSManagedObject
(0x60000057c640) with objectID '0xfa2faad45a7af888
<x-coredata://E8CEB6C1-4881-497F-92D9-4CC2F1AE64B8/Song/
p1>' with oldVersion = 10 and newVersion = 11 and old object
snapshot = {
    album = "<null>";
    composer = "<null>";
    duration = 40;
```

```
    imageURL = "<null>";
    lyrics = "<null>";
    name = "Speak to me";
} and new cached row = {
    album = "<null>";
    composer = "<null>";
    duration = 60;
    imageURL = "<null>";
    lyrics = "<null>";
    name = "Speak to me";
}
)
]
```

We can see that the userInfo describes exactly what objects failed to merge and printed the two versions – the one on the disk and the one that was there when the snapshot was taken.

One option to resolve that is to fix it and try again.

But, as I said, we can also **change the merge policy**, which should be enough in most cases.

Merge Conflict Policy

Optimistic Locking failure requires us to go over the conflicts and make decisions.

Going over the conflicts can be a tough task, but moreover, it may be unnecessary.

In most cases, the decision will be to favor this version or the other. Fortunately, we can define that decision up front when creating our context.

NSManagedObjectContext has a property named mergePolicy, and it describes how to resolve conflicts in our objects.

NSErrorMergePolicy

NSErrorMergePolicy is the default policy for resolving conflicts. It basically means that whenever we have a conflict between the snapshot and the persistent store version, Core Data will throw an error, the one I described in a previous section.

As I said earlier, that is called Optimistic Locking, and you should use that when you don't have situations where your data is being modified from two places simultaneously (otherwise, it's an error).

mergeByPropertyStoreTrump

If you favor external changes over what you have in the persistent store, you should use mergeByPropertyStoreTrump:

```
context.mergePolicy = NSMergePolicy.mergeByPropertyStoreTrump
```

Let's make sure we understand what it means exactly or, rather, what it doesn't mean. It doesn't mean that every external value is saved to the persistent store.

It means that every property that conflicts with the persistent store will override it.

Use this policy whenever you want to favor current user editing, for example.

mergeByPropertyObjectTrump

If you favor the persistent store version, you should use mergeByPropertyObjectTrump:

```
context.mergePolicy = NSMergePolicy. mergeByPropertyObjectTrump
```

This policy is the opposite of the previous one – now, we are favoring the persistent store changes instead.

We probably will use this when we want to favor changes that come from a backend request.

overwrite

When we use the overwrite policy, we save **the entire** in-memory object to the store:

```
context.mergePolicy = NSMergePolicy.overwrite
```

Unlike mergeByPropertyStoreTrump, in this policy, we overwrite every property, even if it doesn't conflict with the store version.

Before using overwrite, notice that this is a very aggressive move, so you should use it carefully.

For example, let's imagine a document that the user is editing. The user has changed the title, and while they were doing that, a new version came from the server with a different title and a different body text.

When the user tries to save the document, they will have a conflict.

The overwrite policy means that not only the title the user modified will be applied to the store but also the "old" body text, even though the user hasn't touched it.

In most cases, we'll use the overwrite policy when there's some meaning for the relationship between the different properties. In other words, the changes in the various properties should go together.

rollback

The rollback policy is the inverse policy of overwrite – in case of a conflict, it ditches every change made in the in-memory version in favor of the store version:

```
context.mergePolicy = NSMergePolicy.rollback
```

We will use the rollback policy when we think that changes made in another place are prioritized over the editing that we are doing now.

Nested Managed Object Contexts

Using multiple object contexts is excellent for some use cases I described earlier.

Another advanced feature of Core Data is the ability to create nested contexts with child/parent relationships.

I know creating a child/parent context relationship may sound scary.

But, while it makes code a little bit more complex, there is a time where it is worth it.

Think about what happens when you want to discard some of the changes that were made by the user, but not all of them.

Or, for example, what happens when validation doesn't pass in some of the changes and then it flunks all the other modifications?

Creating child contexts opens new possibilities to support more sophisticated flows in your app.

What Are Child Contexts?

When we "push" context changes by calling the save() method, we push them to the persistent store coordinator.

Now, if you'll go back and read what I wrote earlier, I said that pushing the changes to the persistent store is what happens **in most cases** (I was careful with my words).

When calling save() in child contexts, instead of pushing changes to the persistent store, Core Data pushes them **to their parent contexts**.

As a matter of fact, child contexts are not even tied to a persistent store – they are entirely dependent on their parent.

Creating a Child Context

Creating a child context is like creating a "regular" context. On second thought, a child context **is a regular** context:

```
let parent = delegate.persistentContainer.viewContext

// creating a new context
let childContext = NSManagedObjectContext(concurrencyType:
.mainQueueConcurrencyType)

// attaching the new context to the parent context
childContext.parent = parent
```

Instead of connecting the new context to the persistent store, we now set its parent property.

Child contexts can also have their own children, and so on. While having a long list of chained contexts won't affect your app performance, it will affect your code complexity, so that's the point when you need to ask yourself, Is it worth it?

In the following chapters, we'll discuss elegant ways to implement Core Data in our apps, so that question will (hopefully) be clearer.

Sync Between Child and Parent

Creating child/parent managed contexts brings up new problems and questions about how changes are being synced between them.

Let's start with this simple statement – changes between a child's and a parent's contexts **can be** synced in two directions.

Look at Figure 5-7.

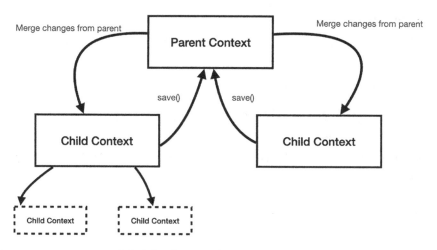

Figure 5-7. *Parent/child relationships*

In Figure 5-7 we can see how child and parent contexts are related.

As I mentioned earlier, calling the save() method in the child context always pushes the changes to its parent.

However, merging the changes down isn't done automatically.

NSManagedObjectContext has a (Boolean) property named automaticallyMergesChangesFromParent. Setting this property to true ensures that parent changes are merged automatically to the child context.

Let's look at the following code:

```
let parentContext = delegate.persistentContainer.viewContext
let childContext1 = NSManagedObjectContext(concurrencyType:
.mainQueueConcurrencyType)
childContext1.parent = parentContext
        childContext1.automaticallyMergesChangesFromParent = true

let childContext2 = NSManagedObjectContext(concurrencyType:
.mainQueueConcurrencyType)
        childContext2.parent = parentContext
        childContext2.automaticallyMergesChangesFromParent = true
```

```
let songInMainContext = NSEntityDescription.
insertNewObject(forEntityName: "Song", into: parentContext)
as! Song
        songInMainContext.name = "Breathe"

let childSong1 = childContext1.object(with: songInMainContext.
objectID) as! Song
let childSong2 = childContext2.object(with: songInMainContext.
objectID) as! Song

childSong1.name = "On the Run"
  try childContext1.save()

  childContext2.refreshAllObjects()
```

The code does something interesting:

- It has a parent context with two child contexts.

- `childContext1` fetches a song, changes its name property, and saves it.

- Following the save action, the change is merged to the parent context.

- After the parent context was updated, the change permeates to `childContext2` automatically, because its `automaticallyMergesChangesFromParent` property is being set to `true`.

- Notice I called `refreshAllObjects()` to ensure the merge action is being done immediately.

The unique relationships between contexts are based on saving and merging and set the ground for another essential aspect of Core Data – concurrency working.

We will talk about concurrency later in the book.

Summary

Learning how to work with contexts is the final piece of the puzzle and lays the ground for more advanced and amazing things with Core Data.

We've learned a lot in this chapter! For example, we've learned

- What are contexts and how to create one

- How to manipulate data – insert, fetch, and delete

- How to define predefined fetch requests in our data model

- How to work with multiple contexts, including Optimistic Locking and merge conflicts

Now it's time to have fun and go deeper into Core Data.

CHAPTER 6

Fetching Data

Programmers waste enormous amounts of time thinking about, or worrying about, the speed of noncritical parts of their programs, and these attempts at efficiency actually have a strong negative impact when debugging and maintenance are considered. We should forget about small efficiencies, say about 97% of the time: premature optimization is the root of all evil.

—Donald Knuth

In the last chapter, we were finally done talking about the Core Data stack, and as promised, we'll now start diving into the deepest secrets of Core Data.

We'll begin with maybe the most important aspect of Core Data – **fetching records**.

I know that we've already learned what NSFetchRequest is or even how to do basic predicates.

But NSPredicate has many more capabilities to offer, and since it's such a central tool, we'll go through most of them now.

In this chapter, we will learn

- The basic NSPredicate syntax, including AND/OR operators

- How to compound predicates

© Avi Tsadok 2022
A. Tsadok, *Unleash Core Data*, https://doi.org/10.1007/978-1-4842-8211-3_6

- How to work with strings and numbers

- How to deal with relationships, including aggregate
  operators, subqueries, and the IN operator

- What debugging tools do we have that work with our
  predicates efficiently

Meet NSPredicate (Again)

As I said in previous chapters, you might be familiar with NSPredicate
from your experience with other frameworks.

NSPredicate holds definitions for both advanced and straightforward
data queries we can do.

Once we create a predicate, we can attach it to a fetch request and
perform the data fetching.

Since NSPredicate is an instance, we can reuse it with other requests
as well.

All predicates are based on formatted strings, making them very simple
and flexible but tricky. Base logic on strings can be a recipe for problems,
and that's something I'll try to address in this chapter.

Creating a basic NSPredicate is simple:

```
let predicate = NSPredicate(format: "name == %@", "Dark Side of
The Moon")
```

It's elementary to understand what the predicate does – it returns all
entities with "name" that equals to the string "Dark Side of The Moon".

But since predicates play a significant role in Core Data usage, there
are much more than that, so let's unleash its power.

Predicate Syntax

There is a couple of stuff we need to know about syntax. First, you should know that predicates are not case sensitive. However, it is customary to uppercase reserved words such as "OR," "NOT," and "AND." In general, using uppercase for reserved words helps developers distinguish them from property names and the rest of the expression.

Using arguments is similar to what you know from string formats. To get more information about it, you can visit the Apple website for an updated reference.

And still, why should we use arguments when we can just include the value within the predicate string?

Going back to the previous example, we can just do that:

```
let predicate = NSPredicate(format: "name == 'Dark Side of
The Moon'")
```

Looks simpler, right?

Well, it is simpler. But using arguments is always safer. For example, look at the "simpler" predicate. You could see I wrapped the name of the album with apostrophes.

Using apostrophes is something NSPredicate is doing for us. Ignoring them may cause our app to crash.

Why did I say "may"? Because when we omit apostrophes, Core Data refers to our value as a native term, such as an entity name or a reserved word.

Theoretically, it can lead to unexpected results or even SQL injection.

So, remember, don't be lazy and always use arguments when possible.

We can also pass an argument for attributes and entity names, but we must use the %K sign.

For example, if we want to rewrite the last predicate with arguments fully, we can do the following:

```
let predicate = NSPredicate(format: "%K == %@", "name",
"Dark Side of The Moon")
```

Trust Core Data knows how to handle that when converting the predicate to a valid SQL query.

If we don't want to pass a string as the key path argument, you can use #keyPath to make it more type-safe:

```
let predicate = NSPredicate(format: "%K == 5", #keyPath(Song.
number))
```

The preceding code will translate the provided key path to a string.

Just look how we easily made the predicate much more type-safe!

AND/OR

Similar to SQL, predicates are able to combine conditions with AND and OR operators, for example:

```
let predicate = NSPredicate(format: "name == %@ AND active ==
%@", "Dark Side of The Moon", false)
```

If you remember from the previous chapter, we can also create AND/OR predicates using the built-in request builder in the data model editor.

Compound Predicates

We can combine not just conditions within a predicate but also predicates.

To do that, we can use a class named NSCompoundPredicate to take an array of predicates and combine them with one of the three operators – AND, OR, NOT.

In the following example, we use the AND compound predicate operator:

```
let filterSongNamePredicate = NSPredicate(format: "name == %@",
"On the Run")
let filterActiveSongsPredicate = NSPredicate(format: "active =
%@", true)
let predicate = NSCompoundPredicate(andPredicateWithSubpredicates:
[filterSongNamePredicate, filterActiveSongsPredicate])
```

One of the great things in `NSCompoundPredicate` is its subclass of NSPredicate. This means we can also combine it with another NSCompoundPredicate and create even more sophisticated predicates:

```
let activeOnTheRunPredicate = NSCompoundPredicate(and
PredicateWithSubpredicates: [filterSongNamePredicate,
filterActiveSongsPredicate])
```

```
let newSongsPredicate = NSPredicate(format: "createdDate > %@",
oneMonthAgo as CVarArg)
```

```
let predicate = NSCompoundPredicate(orPredicateWithSubpredicat
es: [activeOnTheRunPredicate, newSongsPredicate])
```

In the preceding code example, we took the compound predicate we created in the previous example and combined it with a new predicate using the OR operator (`orPredicateWithSubpredicates`).

Hopefully, you will start to see the benefits `NSPredicate` brings to the table. Sure, we can create those queries using some SQL wrapper, but predicates let us reuse queries and make them more modular.

The reusability of the predicates doesn't stop with compound predicates. We can even include variables inside our predicates!

Substitution Variables

Even though predicates use formatted strings with attributes, in the end, it is kind of a "fixed" predicate.

Look at the following predicate from earlier:

```
let predicate = NSPredicate(format: "name == %@", "On the Run")
```

The preceding predicate always filters entities when the "name" attribute equals "On the Run".

Sure, we can reuse this predicate wherever we want, but we can even increase its reusability!

We do that using something called substitution variables:

```
let reusablePredicate = NSPredicate(format: "name == $songName")

let predicate = reusablePredicate.withSubstitutionVariables
(["songName" : "On the Run"])
```

In the preceding example, I declared a variable named songName. We can then pass it in a dictionary with key-value, making the predicate more reusable.

Many developers "recycle" predicates by wrapping them in a function:

```
func getSongsPredicate(byName name : String) -> NSPredicate {
        return NSPredicate(format: "name == %@", name)
}
```

Using "substitution variables" redundant wrapping predicates in functions easily.

Now I want to talk about the type of values we can filter and start with strings.

Working with Strings

Strings play a significant role in databases in general and in Core Data in particular.

The main reason is that, in theory, strings can represent any kind of data – texts, IDs, numbers, JSON, and even binary data.

Core Data has advanced ways to compare strings, similar to what you could find in SQL queries.

Equal

The first and probably the most classic string-related operator is the equal sign, "=":

```
let predicate = NSPredicate(format: "name = %@", name)
```

The equal operator requires the attribute to have the **exact** value as the passed argument.

When browsing different predicate examples, you will probably be going to see the usage of the double equal sign:

```
let predicate = NSPredicate(format: "name == %@", name)
```

Both ways are valid and won't raise an exception.

Now, regarding case-sensitive comparison, when I said that the predicate looks for the exact match, I entirely meant it – the equal operator (and actually all other string operators) is case sensitive.

To make the condition case insensitive, we can add the symbol [c] to the predicate:

```
let predicate = NSPredicate(format: "name == %@[c]", name)
```

You can add the [c] symbol to all string-related operators to make them case insensitive.

Diacritic-Sensitive Comparison

A diacritic, also known as an accent, is a sign added to a letter to give it pronunciation.

You probably know diacritic symbols from Spanish or French.

For example, the word *cómo* in Spanish ("how") has an acute accent.

Now, look at the following code:

```
let predicate = NSPredicate(format: "word == %@[c]", "como") //
will not return "cómo"
```

If there is an entity with a word with the value "cómo", the fetch request will return empty results. That's because "o" and "ó" are different characters.

To overcome this problem, we can add "d" (diacritic) next to the "c" symbol:

```
let predicate = NSPredicate(format: "word == %@[cd]", "como")
// will return "cómo" as well.
```

BEGINSWITH and ENDSWITH

Two additional valuable operators are BEGINSWITH and ENDSWITH. Frankly, their names speak for themselves.

BEGINSWITH searches for strings that begin with the passed argument, and ENDSWITH searches for a string that ends with the given argument:

```
entity.name = "12345"
...
let predicate = NSPredicate(format: "name ENDSWITH %@", "45")
// returns entitiy
let predicate = NSPredicate(format: "name BEGINSWITH %@", "123")
// returns entity
```

And just like the equal operator, we can also add the [cd] symbol to the predicate:

```
let predicate = NSPredicate(format: "name BEGINSWITH[cd] %@",
name) // returns entity
```

LIKE: Wildcard Searches

The LIKE operator gives us tools to create more sophisticated string search queries to provide more flexibility.

If you have SQL experience, a predicate's LIKE is quite similar to the SQL LIKE operator.

Look at the following code:

```
let predicate = NSPredicate(format: "name LIKE %@", name)
// It's like using "="
```

Regarding results, using LIKE is identical to the equal operator, but it might be different performance-wise.

The reason is that the LIKE operator supports wildcard searches.

For example, if we want to search for all words that start with "a" and end with "I", we can represent the middle part with "*":

```
let predicate = NSPredicate(format: "name LIKE %@", "a*I")
// can return "avi", "anni" or "ai"
```

Other than "*", the LIKE operator supports another symbol, "?". The difference between "*" and "?" is that "*" represents 0 or more characters and "?" represents exactly one character.

For example, if we want to search for all names that end with "OM" and have the length of three, we need to do the following:

```
let predicate = NSPredicate(format: "name LIKE %@", "?OM")
// can return "TOM", "BOM" but not "OM" or "BOOM"
```

Using LIKE is excellent when we need to do search predicates to support, well, a search action requested by the user.

In general, LIKE is slower than just using the equal parameter, so don't use it if you don't take advantage of wildcards.

CONTAINS

Another string operator related mainly to searches is CONTAINS.

The CONTAINS operator filters values when they contain the provided argument regarding its position:

```
let predicate = NSPredicate(format: "name CONTAINS %@", "e")
// returns all values that contain the letter "e"
```

In a way, using CONTAINS 'e' is like using LIKE '*e*' and produces the same results.

MATCHES

MATCHES is a special operator used in cases where we need to perform a regular expression search.

The following example searches for alphanumeric values only:

```
let predicate = NSPredicate(format: "name MATCHES %@",
"[a-zA-Z0-9]*")
```

Even if you are not a master in regular expressions, the fact that you're reading this book indicates you know what that is.

The usage of MATCHES is obviously rarer than other operators, but when you need it, it can be compelling.

For example, you can use MATCHES to locate values that start with a number, contain email addresses, or other specific expressions.

Numbers

Most of number-related predicates are straightforward. We can use >, <, <=, and >= like you do in code or in SQL queries:

```
let predicate = NSPredicate(format: "number > %d AND number
< %d", 4, 12)
```

The preceding code returns all values between 4 and 12.

However, one interesting operator you can use to make your life easier is BETWEEN.

BETWEEN can help you filter attributes between two values, just like the preceding code snippet.

The last predicate I showed you is equivalent to the following:

```
let predicate = NSPredicate(format: "number BETWEEN {4, 12}")
```

Another aspect where BETWEEN can be helpful is comparing two Float numbers.

There are cases where Float numbers can be inaccurate. In previous chapters, we saw that we bumped into problems when performing math operations on Float numbers.

Using the BETWEEN operator can help us compare Float numbers in a more reliable way:

```
let predicate = NSPredicate(format: "floatNumber BETWEEN
{0.12, 0.14}") // to compare to 0.13
```

Key Path Collection Queries

Even though collection queries are not part of NSPredicate, they are related to fetching data and can be extremely powerful.

In general, SQLite has some built-in functions that can help us perform aggregation queries.

One classic example would be count, to return the number of items. But we can do even more complex functions such as max, sum, or even calculate average.

However, Core Data predicates don't have aggregation function support.

Another solution we can use is NSExpressionDescription.

Hello, NSExpressionDescription

NSExpressionDescription is one of the advanced features of Core Data that many developers don't become aware of.

Not only are you going to learn about NSExpressionDescription but this will also be a chance to expose you to two additional other features – propertiesToFetch and resultType.

To explain how to aggregate data, I want to start from the end and go back to NSFetchRequest.

As mentioned earlier, NSFetchRequest has two more properties. I'll start with propertiesToFetch.

In propertiesToFetch we can define exactly what properties we want to receive in our fetch request.

Now, properties can be, of course, attributes:

```
fetchRequest.propertiesToFetch = ["title", "duration"]
```

Fetching only two attributes can have a positive influence on performance. But performance optimization is something we will discuss later in the book, so that's not why I show you that right now.

Other than the list of attributes, we can also provide a list of NSPropertyDescription, or in our case NSExpressionDescription, which is one of the NSPropertyDescription subclasses.

In general usage, we work with attributes or relationships. NSExpressionDescription gives us the option to create a new, dynamic, or functional property relevant only to that fetch request.

Creating a New NSExpressionDescription

I know, up until now, we didn't have to write many code lines and enjoy all the goods Core Data has in its sleeves.

But creating a new expression description requires a little bit more extra work.

NSExpressionDescription is built upon NSExpression, which is also made from other expressions.

I want to create a property with the fetched songs' total duration in this example.

I'll start with creating an expression that points to the duration attribute:

```
let keyPathExpression = NSExpression(forKeyPath: "duration")
```

Based on the keyPathExpression, I will now create a summarize expression:

```
let sumDurationExpression = NSExpression(forFunction: "sum:",
arguments: [keyPathExpression])
```

Notice I created an expression based on a function – sum:.

There are more functions we can use, but I'll show you them later, so we can now focus on fetching the songs.

Now that we have an expression that can summarize the songs' duration, we can create a description and add it to the fetch result:

```
let totalDurationDescription = NSExpressionDescription()
totalDurationDescription.name = "totalDuration"
totalDurationDescription.expression = sumDurationExpression

fetchRequest.resultType = .dictionaryResultType
fetchRequest.propertiesToFetch = [totalDurationDescription]
```

There're a couple of new things here. First, we created an
NSExpressionDescription object. The NSExpressionDescription has the
expression we created earlier and has a name – totalDuration. That name
will be the name of the property that returns in the fetch result, which is
part of the reason it is called NSExpression**Description**.

After that, we attach the new expression description to the fetch results
by adding it to the propertiesToFetch array.

If I wanted to visualize the whole thing, I would do something like
Figure 6-1.

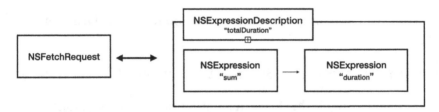

Figure 6-1. *NSExpressionDescription structure*

Even though the code was straightforward up until now, there is one
line that is also new, and that's the **result type**.

When executing a fetch request, we get the results as managed objects.
While that sounds obvious, it's actually the default behavior since we have
more ways to get results.

For example, we can get the result as **managed object IDs** instead of
objects:

```
fetchRequest.resultType = .managedObjectIDResultType
```

When we include the expression description on our list of properties to
fetch, the only result type we can use is dictionaryResultType.

When using dictionaryResultType, we get results as key-value
structures instead of objects.

Executing the fetch request without changing the result will lead to an
exception.

Reusing

Sometimes I feel I'm repeating myself, but the principle of separation of concerns is crucial, so I guess it's worth it to sound like a parrot.

Working with the expression description might sound like a hassle, but when we encapsulate the logic in an object, we can reuse it across our project.

Relationships

After you've learned about relationships and predicates, it's just apparent we know how to integrate them, isn't it?

We need to understand three main things about adding relationship information to our predicates:

1) Relationships in predicates are **being accessed using a key path**, which is a pattern you see more and more in iOS development. Song.album is a way to access an album both in code and predicates.

2) There is a **big difference** between to-one and to-many relationships.

3) When starting to traverse relationships, it's easy to forget the entity that we are fetching. Remember we always fetch one type of entity.

To-One

Let's start with a basic to-one relationship predicate:

```
let predicate = NSPredicate(format: "album.title = %@", "Dark
Side of The Moon")
```

I think that the preceding code is straightforward. What's also nice about the %@ argument is that we can use it to pass not only strings but also managed objects!

Look at that:

```
let predicate = NSPredicate(format: "album = %@", album)
```

If we already fetched the Album instance, that could be a very convenient way to use it as an argument in a predicate.

Now is the time to ask yourself, what's the point? We can just do the following to get album songs:

```
let songs = album.songs
```

And you'll be right. But remember, we can compound predicates and add more conditions to the query.

Now, I want to show you something even more neat.

With the help of key path patterns, relationships can go even deeper. Let's say we have a Library entity with a to-one relationship to Album. Now, I want to fetch all songs from a specific Library, by its name:

```
let predicate = NSPredicate(format: "album.library.name = ",
"My Amazing Library")
```

Now try to do that in an alternative way.

You can chain to-one relationships as much as you want, and Core Data will handle it.

Now, what about to-many?

To-Many

Okay, so fetching objects in a to-one relationship is simple. And it's easy to understand why – we have only one object with one key path to look for.

But what happens when we have a "to-many" relationship?

In this case, things get a little bit more complicated.

There are two ways to filter to-many relationships – aggregate operators and subqueries.

Aggregate Operators

Aggregate operators are probably simpler to include to-many relationships in your predicates.

Let's go back to our Song-Album-Playlist scheme model.

We know that Song->>Playlist is a to-many relationship.

A reminder: It means that a song can be related to multiple playlists, and a playlist can have numerous songs.

Let's try to describe a query in words: We want to fetch **all songs with a playlist named "Top Songs 2021"**.

(If we have multiple playlists with that name, pick them all.)

For that, we can use the aggregate operator ANY:

```
let predicate = NSPredicate(format: "ANY playlists.name = %@",
"Top Songs 2021")
```

Just to focus you, we are fetching songs here, not playlists.

The predicate filters all songs with playlists with their name "Top Songs 2021".

ANY is a really simple and powerful operator, but we can use an additional operator for a to-many relationship – NONE.

As its name stands, NONE filters out songs with playlists that do not comply with the provided condition.

For example, the following predicate returns all songs whose playlists do not have the name "Road Songs":

```
let predicate = NSPredicate(format: "NONE playlists.name = %@",
"Road Songs")
```

ANY and NONE are two helpful operators, but we can move forward to subqueries if we want more power.

SUBQUERY

SUBQUERY is a Core Data tool that many developers are afraid of. It basically means that we can run a **query within a query**.

SUBQUERY is built upon three arguments: the collection name, a variable, and a predicate.

A basic SUBQUERY format looks like this:

```
SUBQUERY(collection name, variable, predicate).@count > 0
```

The collection name is the name of the relationship, and the variable is a name you can choose in the predicate itself.

Confused? Let's rewrite the Song->Playlist example in SUBQUERY:

```
NSPredicate(format: "SUBQUERY(playlists, $playlist, $playlist.
name ==[cd] %@).@count > 0", "Top Songs 2021")
```

- The collection is the `Playlists` relationship.

- `$playlist` is the variable we use inside the predicate itself. We can use any name we want.

- The predicate takes the playlist variable and compares it to "Top Songs 2021".

Now, the obvious question might be, Why should we use SUBQUERY when ANY and NONE are doing the job perfectly?

And that's a good question. In most cases, ANY and NONE are doing a great job, but there are rare cases where they cannot do what SUBQUERY can. And these are the cases where SUBQUERY comes in hand.

Do you want to see an example? No problem.

Let's try to add another condition to our query. We want to fetch songs that are not only in a playlist named "Top Songs 2021" but also in playlists owned by a specific email.

Let's try to do that with an aggregate operator:

```
let predicate = NSPredicate(format: "ANY playlists.name = %@
AND ANY playlists.ownerEmail = %@", "Top Songs 2021", "myemail@
mydoamain.com")
```

Who needs SUBQUERY, ha?

The preceding predicate returns songs that have a playlist named "Top Songs 2021" and songs that are owned by myemail@mydomain.com, but the problem is that according to ANY, they don't have to be the same playlist!

It's clearly not what we want.

The proper way to do that is by using a multi-condition SUBQUERY:

```
NSPredicate(format: "SUBQUERY(playlists, $playlist, $playlist.
name ==[cd] %@ AND $playlist.ownerEmail = %@).@count > 0", "Top
Songs 2021", "myemail@mydoamain.com")
```

We know how to build a predicate. SUBQUERY lets us run the predicate on a to-many relationship inside another predicate, and that's a difference from ANY.

IN

Another handy operator you need to add to your toolbox is IN.

IN, similar to SQL IN, filters on argument by checking if it exists in a closed list of values:

```
let numbers = [1,2,3,4,5]
let predicate = NSPredicate(format: "number IN %@", numbers)
```

The preceding code snippet is pretty simple – we create an array of numbers and check that "<number> IN <list of numbers>".

IN can be used not just when filtering arguments but also with relationships.

For example, here is a usage for a to-one relationship:

```
let albums = [darkSideOfTheMoon, theWall]
let predicate = NSPredicate(format: "album IN %@", albums)
```

The predicate returns all songs in the two albums mentioned.

We can even use IN for to-many relationships:

```
let playlists = [myTopSongs, topSongsOf60]
let predicate = NSPredicate(format: "ANY playlists IN %@",
playlists)
```

Notice I've used the ANY operator in this predicate. You should already be familiar with that operator when we discussed aggregate operators. You should also remember to add the ANY operator in to-many relationships. Running the predicate without an aggregate operator will return empty results.

Another interesting keyword to be used with the IN operator is SELF. SELF refers to each object checked in the query, for example:

```
let predicate = NSPredicate(format: "SELF IN %@", songs)
// results equal to..songs?
```

I know that code snippet looks kind of...silly. Running it will return, well, the same songs list we just passed.

But SELF with IN can be helpful in use cases where we want to run a predicate and filter it from a closed list of objects.

For example, here's a code snippet to get songs created after a certain date and belonging to a list of songs:

```
let predicate = NSPredicate(format: "creationData > %@ AND SELF
IN %@", date, mySongs)
```

Note   Some of the predicates I show here can be used on an array, regardless of Core Data. That's fine! I can give you the toolset and use cases, but it's up to you to decide how to implement them.

Debugging

Reading a book chapter about predicates is excellent for learning. But we all know once we get into code, things may get more complicated.

Modifying your predicates, recompiling your project, and viewing the results can be frustrating.

Let's start with the bottom line – writing unit tests when dealing with Core Data predicates is extremely helpful, and it's a win-win move since you also have ongoing testing for your code.

I'm putting unit tests aside for now – we'll have a whole maintenance chapter to discuss it.

Also, I want to focus on predicate debugging – not performance.

There are several essential tools to debug your Core Data predicates: using the console, launch arguments, external data editor, and Playgrounds.

Console

That may find you in shock, but using the console is one of the quickest and popular ways to check your predicates.

I find it hard to believe some developers are not aware of using the console for debugging, but I'll straighten things up first anyway.

Basically, we can set a breakpoint in our app and run Swift commands straight from the console, with the context of our app.

That capability allows us to run predicates on our persistent store easily.

We can run Swift/Obj-C code using the command PO.

To make things easier and simpler, it is better to create functions to help you.

For example, imagine a function that returns objects by a predicate, something like this:

```
func getItems(withPredicate predicate : NSPredicate) ->
[NSManagedObject] { ... }
```

Now, we can run a console command to check what returns:

```
po getItems(withPredicate: NSPredicate(format: "ANY playlists.
name = %@", "p1"))
```

And of course, we can play with the predicate and run the command repeatedly without recompiling until we get the expected results.

Of course, evaluating code in the console is relevant not only to handle Core Data predicates but also for other debugging issues. Core Data predicates have trial-and-error sessions, so they are a perfect fit for that technique.

Launch Arguments

Another tool we can use is launching the app with an argument that can help you see how the Core Data framework works under the hood and how it runs SQL commands.

To reveal that secret tool, open the scheme editor (Product ➤ Scheme ➤ Edit Scheme, Figure 6-2).

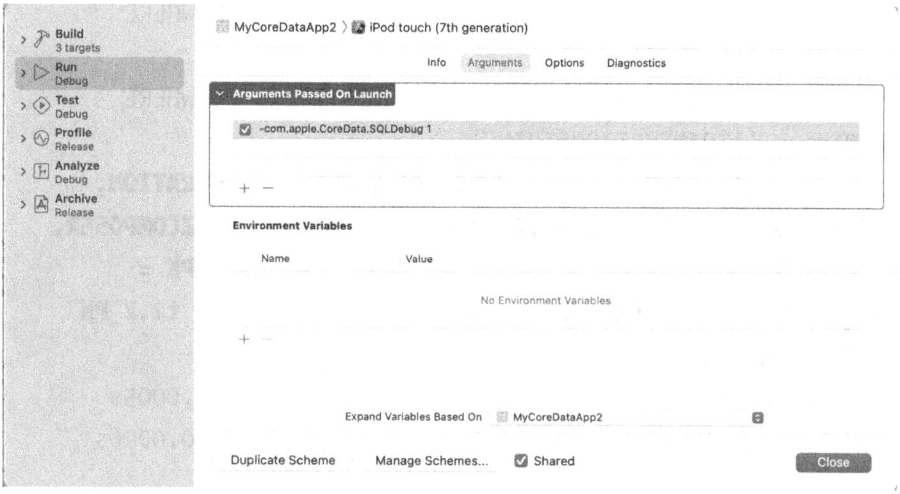

Figure 6-2. *Scheme editor*

Under Run ➤ Arguments ➤ Arguments Passed On Launch, you can see a list of arguments that are passed to your app when it launches.

Add the following argument:

```
-com.apple.CoreData.SQLDebug 1
```

Now, rerun your app and look at your console.

You are supposed to see lines similar to the following:

```
CoreData: sql: SELECT TBL_NAME FROM SQLITE_MASTER WHERE
TBL_NAME = 'Z_METADATA'
CoreData: sql: pragma recursive_triggers=1
CoreData: sql: pragma journal_mode=wal
CoreData: sql: SELECT Z_VERSION, Z_UUID, Z_PLIST FROM
Z_METADATA
CoreData: sql: SELECT TBL_NAME FROM SQLITE_MASTER WHERE
TBL_NAME = 'Z_METADATA'
CoreData: sql: SELECT TBL_NAME FROM SQLITE_MASTER WHERE
TBL_NAME = 'Z_MODELCACHE'
```

```
CoreData: sql: SELECT TBL_NAME FROM SQLITE_MASTER WHERE
TBL_NAME = 'ACHANGE'
CoreData: sql: SELECT TBL_NAME FROM SQLITE_MASTER WHERE
TBL_NAME = 'ATRANSACTIONSTRING'
CoreData: sql: SELECT 0, t0.Z_PK, t0.Z_OPT, t0.ZDURATION,
t0.ZIMAGEURL, t0.ZNAME, t0.ZNUMBER, t0.ZALBUM, t0.ZCOMPOSER,
t0.ZLYRICS FROM ZSONG t0 JOIN Z_4SONGS t1 ON t0.Z_PK =
t1.Z_5SONGS JOIN ZPLAYLIST t2 ON t1.Z_4PLAYLISTS = t2.Z_PK
WHERE  t2.ZNAME = ?
CoreData: annotation: sql connection fetch time: 0.0005s
CoreData: annotation: total fetch execution time: 0.0006s
for 0 rows.
```

The output you see in the console gives you a detailed list of actions that happened in your Core Data, including connections and SQL queries executed.

Now, don't worry about the table naming and structure. We will cover that later, but you can still see exactly what's going on under the hood (I marked the critical part).

If you're getting weird results, console debugging might be an excellent place to start with.

Playgrounds

Another great tool to use is Swift Playgrounds.

Even though you probably know what Playgrounds is, I will briefly talk about it.

Playgrounds is a tool provided by Xcode that lets you play with Swift code outside your app or any project to try and learn stuff related to Swift and development in general.

Add a Playground

Can I assume you already have a project configured with Core Data and a data model?

Great, we can move on. If not, please set up one. You are already supposed to know how to do that.

Now go to File ➤ New ➤ Playground. Select a blank template (see Figure 6-3).

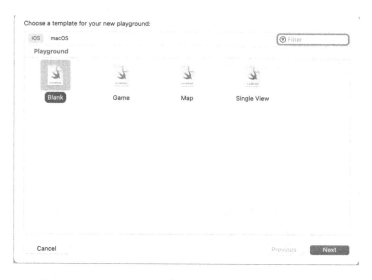

Figure 6-3. *Selecting a template for our playground*

After selecting a template, you need to choose a location for your playground. Save the new playground inside the project.

Let's Play

Now we can start playing with our data:

```
import UIKit
import CoreData

let appDeleate = AppDelegate()
appDelegate.persistentContainer.viewContext
let context = appDeleate.persistentContainer.viewContext

// adding some data
let song = NSEntityDescription.insertNewObject(forEntityName:
"Song", into: context) as! Song
song.name = "My Song"

try! context.save()

// fetch data
let fetchRequest = NSFetchRequest<Song>(entityName: "Song")
fetchRequest.predicate = NSPredicate(format: "name = %@", "My Song")
let result = try! context.fetch(fetchRequest)
print(result.count)
```

I added a new Song instance to our data store in the preceding example and fetched it back using a predicate.

Now I can rerun the playground code quickly and try new predicates and configurations.

However, here are some key points you need to be aware of:

- To start, not only is Playgrounds not an ap but it's also not a part of your app bundle. This means that Playgrounds doesn't have access to your App Delegate and has its own App Delegate. If you reference the persistent container in the App Delegate, that's something you should address.

- It is best to use the **in-memory store type** when playing with Playgrounds. Just like testing, we should start from scratch with every run. You can add a parameter to your Core Data setup so you can initiate to work with the in-memory store when you're on Playgrounds.

- Don't hesitate to create other playgrounds that handle different Core Data checkouts. That's what they are for!

To summarize, Playgrounds is an excellent tool for Core Data feature discovery and is easy to set up.

External Data Editor

The previous tools I mentioned are great. But I think that as a developer, you might have noticed something crucial is missing – the ability actually to view your store data.

Personally, I think Apple should provide a built-in tool in their Simulator or as a separate app that can view, track, and edit data in Core Data stores.

Since there isn't any built-in tool that can do that, some developers have created their own external tool to let you view your app data.

These tools are based on two components of the stack – **the model scheme file** and the **persistent store file** (in this case, SQLite file). The third stack layer, which is the context, is created in the tool itself to complete the stack.

One recommended tool you can use is "Core Data Lab" (`https://betamagic.nl/products/coredatalab.html`), which saves you the hassle of tracking the model and SQLite files and does that for you (Figure 6-4).

Figure 6-4. *Core Data Lab, taken from their website*

Of course, many other tools do the same job. If you get serious about keeping a large data store, picking one of them would be a good move.

Summary

So we've learned how to deal with predicates in different ways – strings, numbers, and relationships.

We also learned how to debug predicates in a variety of techniques.

In the next chapter, we will learn how to implement Core Data in our app – not just set it up but combine it with our day-to-day classes and structs.

CHAPTER 7

Implementation

Simplicity, carried to the extreme, becomes elegance.

—Jon Franklin

Until now, we've been discussing Core Data stack setup techniques, inserting data, and fetching.

But this book is not only about the technical details but also about practical usage and methodology.

In this chapter, we will focus on how to implement Core Data in our daily usage as app developers:

- – How to set the boundaries for Core Data in our app

- – What is DTO (data transfer object) and how it works with Core Data

- – How to observe store changes and update our UI

- – What is `NSFetchedResultsController`

- – How UndoManager works

© Avi Tsadok 2022
A. Tsadok, *Unleash Core Data*, https://doi.org/10.1007/978-1-4842-8211-3_7

Boundaries and Separations

Before we dive into the Core Data implementation, we first need to decide **the boundaries** of the framework in our app and the layers we think Core Data should live in.

A typical iOS app has three main layers:

- Data/network layer

- Business logic layer

- UI layer

The layer that includes Core Data really depends on our perspective on isolating data in our projects.

Isolation

For example, one way to integrate Core Data in our projects is to isolate it from the rest of the app.

We can encapsulate Core Data in one component, and that component is the only one that "knows" what Core Data is.

I tried to demonstrate that in Figure 7-1.

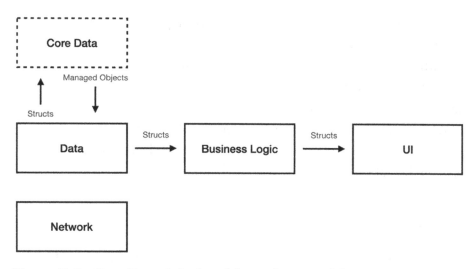

Figure 7-1. *Core Data is isolated from the rest of the app*

Isolating Core Data means that whenever a data entity leaves the Core Data unit, **it's being converted** to some struct or any other abstracted form and passed on to the rest of the app. The opposite goes when data enters the Core Data unit – it is converted back from the abstracted form to a managed object and then saved back to the data store.

This technique has several significant pros:

- Our app **is not "based"** on Core Data. We can theoretically switch to another form of data layer without doing significant modifications to our codebase.

- We are not dependent on the attributes we defined in Core Data in the first place – the structure that is passed on **can be anything we like** and has the potential to make our life easier.

- Even though Core Data provides excellent tools for **concurrency** and editing data using contexts, in a way, this technique simplifies the problem and gives you more flexibility.

But isolating Core Data from the rest of the app also has some drawbacks.

Putting aside all the great features Core Data has in its sleeves - the major problem with that pattern circles around a critical aspect of data and state management - keeping **one source of truth**.

Whenever we convert managed objects to other types of entities, we are practically making copies of our data, which can lead to sync issues between the data store and the rest of the app.

Protocols

So what should be our strategy? We want to encapsulate the Core Data layer, but at the same time, we want to enjoy its features and comply with the essential single source of truth principle.

So another approach is to **abstract the objects** with protocols. Protocols are a great way to give an object a different "identity" while preserving its functionality and content.

In the following code, I added a protocol named "SongProtocol" that has similar properties to the original Song managed object.

The Song entity conforms to that protocol and, by that, is "hidden" under a different name:

```
protocol SongProtocol {

    var name: String? { get set }
    var duration: Float { get set }
}

extension Song: SongProtocol { }
```

Of course, I took the simple and easy path - I named the protocol "SongProtocol" and added the exact same properties as the original. But we can define whatever properties we want and under the hood point their get/set to the "real" attributes.

Protocols provide us flexibility and at the same time keep our source of truth principle.

Core Data Everywhere

If we want to flip over to the other side of the discussion, we can use Core Data basically in every layer of our app.

Even though Core Data is coupled with our codebase, it still has some significant advantages.

The Core Data framework provides valuable tools for binding our data to the UI layer, network requests, and even managing editing changes done by the user.

In the end, as a developer, you need to decide where you want to cross the line between your project and Core Data – do you want to **decouple** your code and give up some of the Core Data capabilities or increase **coupling** and enjoy them?

After this chapter, let's hope you'll have the tools to decide.

Now, let's talk about networking and Core Data.

Network Objects

Almost all projects that implement Core Data also make network requests.

Moreover, most of them sync models they get from network requests to Core Data managed objects and vice versa.

In other words, many times, we want our Core Data store to correlate the relevant piece of data the user has on our server.

Even though I was uncertain, I chose to start with network requests because that's how our data flows – from the back end to the UI layer.

So what's the right way to manage that?

Meet DTOs: Data Transfer Objects

When talking about data, there are several types of data objects.

To understand what DTO is, we should go over the different types of data objects we may bump into:

- *Value Objects* – A small object that contains data

- *Data Access Object* – An object that provides easy access to a persistent store

- *Business Object* – Combines business logic and entities

- *Data Transfer Object* – An object that helps transfer data in different processes

Confused? That's understandable.

If we want to assign a data object to a role in our app, we can think of data access objects as Core Data managed objects. Value objects containing small data such as locations, addresses, positions, and states can be part of the view model.

A business object can be some logic object we can put in our business logic layer.

But what are data transfer objects (DTOs)?

When working with network requests, we usually have an API that requires us to work with a specific format.

There are two ways to handle that:

- We can read the network response **as a dictionary** and update/create our Core Data entity by looping the dictionary keys.

- We can encode the network response **as a struct** and map the struct to a Core Data entity.

Those structs we create just to encode/decode the data are called DTOs.

Creating DTOs

A DTO is usually a struct that conforms to the Codable protocol.

A Song DTO can look something like this:

```
struct SongDTO: Codable {

    let name: String?
    let duration: Float
}
```

The DTO structure can be either the same format as our managed objects or different, but what's more important is that it needs to be the format the server requires or returns.

A mapping function can be something like this:

```
extension Song {

    func updateFrom(songDTO : SongDTO) {
        self.name = songDTO.name
        self.duration = songDTO.duration
    }
}
```

Let's Make It Dynamic

Senior developers should move uncomfortably in their chair with the code snippet I provided.

Its main drawback is that every time we add or change something in our Core Data model, we need to update the DTO mapping code.

And that manual mapping feels even more awkward when we realize the properties even have **the same name**! No way it can't be done automatically, is it?

Well, we can make it automatically, and for that magic to happen, we need two capabilities: on one hand **reflection** and on the other hand **entity description**.

Reflection

If we want to dynamically update the Core Data entity, we need to go over our DTO properties without knowing them in compile time.

We can do just that using something called "reflection."

Reflection is a process where we can examine (or even modify) a specific structure or a class.

Look at how I run reflection on SongDTO:

```
let mirror = Mirror(reflecting: songDTO)
for child in mirror.children {
    let label = child.label
    let value = child.value
}
```

The label is our property name, and the value is its value.

Going back to the beginning of our book, now it seems easy to map values back to our entity:

```
extension Song {

    func update(from songDTO: SongDTO) {
        let mirror = Mirror(reflecting: songDTO)
        for child in mirror.children {
            if let label = child.label {
                self.setValue(child.value, forKeyPath: label)
            }
        }
    }
}
```

Simple, right?

You should be aware that the preceding code is very basic. It won't work when we have different types, different names, or relationships of any kind.

To enhance our mapping process, we need to do additional work. Since we have full access to entity and attribute descriptions, we can do anything we want.

To summarize the process, look at Figure 7-2.

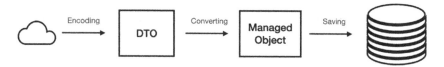

Figure 7-2. *Saving data from the network to Core Data*

DTO is a recommended design pattern that lets us separate our data from the API back end by creating a "bridge" the handles all the conversions.

We can even make it dynamic if we want and make the process more stable and easy to maintain.

Working with the UI Layer

Previously we talked about one side of our app – reading network requests and saving them to our Core Data.

Now let's discuss the other side – the UI layer.

What Do We Want?

Basically, we want our UI components to be updated **whenever our data store changes** (whether it's in memory or persistent) to provide our users with a seamless experience.

It's also logical to connect that experience to what we just learned – update data from network requests (Figure 7-3).

Backend   Core Data Store   UI Layer

Figure 7-3. *Update the UI from network requests*

We have several techniques we can choose from, and we can even combine them to make it happen.

Observing Data Changes Using Notifications

Perhaps the most basic way to perform updates to our UI is to observe changes in our Core Data using the familiar notification center design pattern:

```
NotificationCenter.default.addObserver(self, selector:
#selector(dataChanged(notif:)), name: NSManagedObjectContext.
didChangeObjectsNotification, object: nil)
```

didChangeObjectsNotification is called whenever a context is being saved, and the notification that is being sent contains detailed information about the changes that occurred.

The expression "a context is being saved" should raise some eyebrows. What context? We can have multiple contexts. Does it also mean our persistent store was updated too?

Let's break things up.

The received notification contains a userInfo object with the following information:

- List of inserted objects

- List of deleted objects

- List of updated objects

Also, in this case, the notification object is the managed object context that was changed.

What we need to do now is to understand the change and respond accordingly.

How to Respond

As said earlier, when the didChangeObjectsNotification notification is called, the notification object itself is the context that was saved. In most cases, what we care about is the **UI to be updated**.

Therefore, we can check whether the context that was sent with the notification is the view context:

```
@objc func dataChanged(notif: NSNotification) {
    guard let context = notif.object as?
    NSManagedObjectContext,
    let delegate = UIApplication.shared.delegate as?
    AppDelegate else {
        return
    }

    if context == delegate.persistentContainer.
    viewContext {
        // UI context
    }
}
```

Checking the type of context that was saved ensures we don't refresh our screen for no reason and make extra work.

But even here, things may become trickier. What if we get a notification the view context was being saved, but it **has nothing to do** with our current UI screen? Maybe the change was in an attribute that doesn't affect our screen? Or even worse, what if it happens in an object that we don't care about at the moment?

We have the option to dig into the userInfo, analyze it, and understand whether we need to reload our UI, but this can be a frustrating task to understand if we need to reload our screen.

Lucky us, Apple has a better solution for us.

NSFetchedResultsController

Many Core Data–based apps use table or collection views to display data. You know what? The same goes for many non-Core Data–based apps as well.

Table/collection views are great controls that can easily handle a large amount of data.

When the collection data is connected to a Core Data stack, it requires a **stable and efficient** mechanism of fetching and refreshing data.

Using what I previously showed you, we can write that mechanism ourselves using notifications to observe data changes, rebuild our data structure, and perform the changes in our table view.

The other option is to use NSFetchedResultsController, provided by the Core Data framework, to handle precisely these kinds of cases.

What Is It Exactly?

To simplify the explanation, you can think of NSFetchedResultsController as an instance linked to a fetch request on one side and a table/collection view on the other side.

NSFetchedResultsController has several capabilities we can take advantage of:

- Fetching the data for the collection view

- Dividing the data into sections and rows

- Responding to data changes

- Managing cache

Creating an NSFetchedResultsController

Let's continue with our excellent music app of songs, albums, and playlists.

In our app, we want to create a Library screen. The "Library" screen must display all the songs the user has been saving, grouped by albums.

We are going to start with creating a fetch request:

```
let fetchRequest = Song.fetchRequest()
fetchRequest.sortDescriptors = [NSSortDescriptor(key: "name",
ascending: false)]
```

As you can see, creating the fetch request is followed by **adding a sort descriptor**.

In the case of NSFetchedResultsController, adding a sort descriptor is mandatory. A sort descriptor is required because **we cannot display a different ordering** each time we refresh the fetch results. The resulting order becomes even more critical when deleting or inserting new objects.

Based on the fetch request we have just created, we can now move on and create the **FRC** (NS**F**etched**R**esults**C**ontroller):

```
fetchController = NSFetchedResultsController(fetchRe
quest: fetchRequest, managedObjectContext: context,
sectionNameKeyPath: nil, cacheName: nil)
```

Besides the fetch request, there are additional parameters we can or need to provide when initializing the FRC.

First, we need to provide a **managed object context** the NSFetchedResultsController will work with.

Even though the NSFetchedResultsController is relevant to UI-related tasks only, you need to remember that we can work with multiple main contexts or even multiple stacks.

Just like the fetch request, the context parameter is **mandatory**.

The rest of the parameters are not mandatory, but they add additional capabilities.

With sectionNameKeyPath, we can help the FRC group the results into sections that answer many TableView needs.

The cacheName can help the FRC optimize its fetching mechanism, making it more efficient when handling a big amount of data.

Both sectionNameKeyPath and cacheName parameters will be discussed soon, I promise!

After setting the fetch request, we need to call performFetch() to start up the NSFetchedResultsController and load it with objects:

```
try fetchController.performFetch()
```

Now our NSFetchedResultsController is loaded, and we can connect it to our table view (or UICollectionView, for that matter).

Connect the NSFetchedResultsController

The first rule: When we create the FRC (again NSFetchedResultsController), we need to use it **everywhere on the screen** – as it keeps track of all the objects, the number of sections, and rows.

The FRC has dedicated functions to help you fill your table views with content.

Let's look how they fit in when implementing UITableView data source functions:

```
func numberOfSections(in tableView: UITableView) -> Int {
      return fetchController.sections?.count ?? 0
   }

func tableView(_ tableView: UITableView, numberOfRowsInSection
section: Int) -> Int {
      let sectionInfo = fetchController.sections![section]
      return sectionInfo.numberOfObjects
   }

func tableView(_ tableView: UITableView, cellForRowAt
indexPath: IndexPath) -> UITableViewCell {
      let cell = tableView.dequeueReusableCell(with
      Identifier: "SongCell")!
      let object = fetchController.object(at: indexPath)
      cell.textLabel?.text = object.name
      return cell
}
```

Note   If you don't know how table views work, now is the time to lay down the book and learn. It's an essential component and should be basic knowledge by now.

There are two new things here. First, in the cellForRow function, we have a function that returns an object by its indexPath:

```
let object = fetchController.object(at: indexPath)
```

In the other two functions, we make use of the FRC `sections` property:

```
let sectionInfo = fetchController.sections![section]
        return sectionInfo.numberOfObjects
```

It's like FRC was created just for that! (Actually, that is precisely what FRC was made for.)

As promised, now I want to explain how sections work in FRC.

Sections

FRC can group our objects in sections using a critical path we provide. Even though it's an optional feature, it is extremely powerful and valuable.

For example, if we want every section to be the song's album name, we can pass the album name as the key path when initializing the NSFetchedResultsController:

```
fetchController = NSFetchedResultsController(fetchRe
quest: fetchRequest, managedObjectContext: context,
sectionNameKeyPath: #keyPath(Song.album.title), cacheName: nil)
```

```
func tableView(_ tableView: UITableView,
titleForHeaderInSection section: Int) -> String? {
        let sectionInfo = fetchController.sections![section]
        return sectionInfo.name
    }
```

And the results are like magic (Figure 7-4).

Figure 7-4. *Sections according to the album title*

But sections don't have to be according to an attribute; it can be **any key path we want**.

For example, let's say we want our table view to display the songs grouped by their first letter.

First, we need to create a new Song computed variable that returns its name first character:

```
extension Song {

    @objc var prefix: String {
        return String(self.name!.prefix(1))
    }
}
```

And then, we can use the prefix variable as a key path when initializing our FRC:

```
NSFetchedResultsController(fetchRequest: fetchRequest,
managedObjectContext: context, sectionNameKeyPath:
#keyPath(Song.prefix), cacheName: nil)
```

Now our songs are grouped differently (Figure 7-5).

Figure 7-5. *Group songs by their prefix*

What can we learn from that? That grouping by sections can be smarter than using "dump" data – we can use computed variables. That capability provides us the flexibility to do something we previously had to handle ourselves.

Respond to Changes

Remember we need to pass a Core Data context to our NSFetchedResultsController?

Until now, whenever that context changed, we had to call the tableView `reloadData()` method to refresh our screen.

The FRC has a solution just for that – a delegate that can inform us each time our data changes.

But it doesn't end here.

The FRC is brilliant – updating us when the context has changed isn't good enough. FRC informs us every time **the results for our fetch request** have changed. Suppose an entity unrelated to our fetch request has changed. In that case, the delegate method won't be called, and that is one significant advantage FRC has over previous techniques such as observing general notifications.

Now let's meet `NSFetchedResultsControllerDelegate`.

To set it up, we need to connect the delegate to our fetch controller the same as we do with most delegates:

```
fetchController.delegate = self
```

To enable change tracking, we need to implement one of the delegate methods.

Once we do that, we have two options to update our UI – the "new" way or the "old" way.

beginUpdates( ) and endUpdates( )

Since iOS 13 (where SwiftUI and diffable data sources were introduced), refreshing a table view (or a collection view for that matter) using `beginUpdates()` and `endUpdates()` is considered to be the **"old way."**

But the "old way" is still relevant, and FRC fully supports it.

A reminder: To refresh a table, we need to

- Call `beginUpdate()` before the change.

- Make the changes in our data source.

- Make the changes in the tableView by calling insert, update, and delete.

- Call endUpdate().

Before the changes are about to proceed, FRC calls the following delegate method:

```
func controllerWillChangeContent(_ controller: NSFetchedResults
Controller<NSFetchRequestResult>) {
    tableView.beginUpdates()
}
```

As a result, we can add the beginUpdates() method.

To handle data changes, FRC calls the didChange method:

```
func controller(_ controller: NSFetchedResultsController<NS
FetchRequestResult>, didChange anObject: Any, at indexPath:
IndexPath?, for type: NSFetchedResultsChangeType, newIndexPath:
IndexPath?) {
    switch (type) {
    case .insert:
        if let indexPath = newIndexPath {
            tableView.insertRows(at: [indexPath], with: .fade)
        }
        break;
    case .delete:
        if let indexPath = indexPath {
            tableView.deleteRows(at: [indexPath], with: .fade)
        }
        break;
    case .update:
        if let indexPath = indexPath, let cell = tableView.
        cellForRow(at: indexPath) {
```

```
            configureCell(cell, at: indexPath)
        }
        break;
    case .move:
        if let indexPath = indexPath {
            tableView.deleteRows(at: [indexPath], with: .fade)
        }

        if let newIndexPath = newIndexPath {
            tableView.insertRows(at: [newIndexPath],
            with: .fade)
        }
        break;
    }
}
```

As you can see, the didChange method does all the dirty work of understanding exactly what happened to our data.

The method is called for every object that was changed and provides us information on what happens, to whom, and where.

All we need to do is respond correctly and roll out the changes in our table view.

An additional interesting delegate method you should be familiar with is didChange sectionInfo:

```
func controller(_ controller: NSFetchedResultsContr
oller<NSFetchRequestResult>, didChange sectionInfo:
NSFetchedResultsSectionInfo, atSectionIndex sectionIndex: Int,
for type: NSFetchedResultsChangeType)
```

This method provides you with information similar to the previous method but related to sections.

Even though FRC handles the "old way" changes, let's move on to the "new way."

Starting with iOS 13, Apple introduced "diffable data sources" to handle collection view and table view changes.

Fortunately, Apple also updated NSFetchedResultsController to support diffable data sources as well.

Diffable Data Source

One of the primary problems with updating table views and collection views is to **figure out the differences** in our data source to tell the collection exactly what has changed.

Once our data source and collection are not synced together, our app will get an exception and crash.

Diffable data sources introduced in iOS 13 solved that problem for us, and collection data refresh is made very simple and stable.

All we need to do is provide a new data snapshot, and that's it.

Note   If you are not familiar with how a diffable data source works, go to Apple's website or search the Web for extra information. It's a leap forward from how we made changes in the past.

The way NSFetchedResultsController handles diffable data sources is even simpler than the beginUpdate()/endUpdate() way.

Because all the changes, sections, and rows are encapsulated in a data snapshot, FRC provides us with a new data snapshot:

```
func controller(_ controller: NSFetchedResultsController
<NSFetchRequestResult>, didChangeContentWith snapshot:
NSDiffableDataSourceSnapshot<SectionType, ItemType>) {
        dataSource.apply(snapshot, animatingDifferences: true)
    }
```

That's it? Yes! See how simple it is?

Binding our data to our collections has been made simpler.

One additional delegate method that is good to know is

```
func controller(_ controller: NSFetchedResultsController
<NSFetchRequestResult>, didChangeContentWith diff: Collection
Difference<NSManagedObjectID>)
```

The didChangeContentWith method provides us a "semiautomatic" way of updating our collections as it gives us information about changes between two collections. I called it "semiautomatic" because, unlike the snapshot object, here we get the raw data of changes and can decide what to do with it.

Notice that this method works only if we don't implement didChangeContentWith snapshot and it also doesn't support section key path.

Caching

Even though NSFetchedResultsController is very efficient, it's still working under the laws of physics.

When handling a large amount of data (let's say 10,000+ objects), we may experience performance issues.

When creating an NSFetchedResultsController, one of the parameters we haven't discussed yet is cacheName:

```
fetchController = NSFetchedResultsController(fetchRe
quest: fetchRequest, managedObjectContext: context,
sectionNameKeyPath: nil, cacheName: "myCache")
```

Just a reminder of what a cache is: "A component that stores data so that future requests for that data can be served faster, and it might the results of previous computation."

To set up a cache for our FRC, we need to provide a **unique name** during the initialization (look at the preceding code sample).

What happens now is very simple:

- When the `NSFetchedResultsController` asked to fetch data for the first time, it fetched it and saved the results in a cache file with the name provided in the `init()` function.

- The next time `NSFetchedResultsController` will be asked to fetch data from the store, Core Data will check **if the data in the cache file is still valid**. Instead of computing the sections and order, it takes that information from the cache file.

- If the cache is not valid, Core Data will delete the cache file, compute the fetch request, and resave the cache file.

What is considered to be a "valid cache"?

Core Data checks to see if the data store has changed since it saved the cache (by comparing the timestamp).

If Core Data finds the cache valid, the data will be loaded very quickly.

Because caching is based on a persistent file, it is still there when the user kills the app and loads it again.

Not only that, the cache is relevant even if the Core Data store is shared with another extension.

Delete the Cache

There's one small catch with cache (try to tell it five times in a row).

The cache that saves serialized data is in a specific format, derived from the predicate we used for the fetch request.

Once we change the fetch request, we cannot use the existing cache file.

It might happen when we release a new version of our app, with modifications to our fetch request while the user already has a cache file with a different structure.

In this case, the app may crash with the following error:

```
*** Terminating app due to uncaught exception
'NSInternalInconsistencyException', reason: 'FATAL ERROR:
The persistent cache of section information does not match
the current configuration.  You have illegally mutated the
NSFetchedResultsController's fetch request, its predicate, or
its sort descriptor without either disabling caching or using
+deleteCacheWithName:'
```

We have two ways of handling this situation:

- We need to delete the cache using the deleteCache(withName:) static method on version upgrade. Deleting the cache requires us to understand that the app was updated.

- Give the cache a new name, ignoring the old file.

The second way sounds much more straightforward, and I would recommend going with it.

To summarize, cache won't help your NSFetchedResultsController fetching its data from the store faster on the initial fetching.

But, for a large amount of data, things will be much faster on the next loads as long as the request and data don't change frequently.

Undo

Like NSFetchedResultsController, the undo mechanism is another feature we get for free when we implement Core Data in our app.

Yes, Core Data has a built-in undo mechanism!

In fact, the undo feature has been part of Core Foundation and has been an integral part of OS X from its early days.

Since Core Data context's primary goal is to track changes in the data model, it's just natural for Apple to integrate its undo library right into Core Data.

Why Do I Need It?

In most cases, you won't. I mean, it really depends on what you are working on.

Generally, the undo feature is related to a relevant UI flow, for example, an editor screen where the user can add more elements and has the ability to regret and "undo" their last actions.

Meet UndoManager

Core Data undo is very simple. How simple? There's one object you should know, and that's the UndoManager.

To enable undo, all you need to do is create an UndoManager and connect it to your context:

```
let undoManager = UndoManager()
context.undoManager = undoManager
```

The undo tracking begins once we set the UndoManager property in our context.

UndoManager has some basic actions we can use.

We can delete the last action on our context:

```
context.undoManager?.undo()
```

And we can also redo:

```
context.undoManager?.redo()
```

If you connect an Undo button tap event to the redo/undo actions and update your UI as needed, you'll get the familiar classic user experience like other apps you know.

Grouping

If you're thinking to yourself that the UndoManager is something you'll probably use only once, wait for that – you can group actions and undo/redo the whole group together.

Grouping means that one undo operation removes a group of actions. Why do we need that?

There are cases where object modifications need to be coupled with additional changes.

For example, imagine an illustration app with documents with UI elements the user can edit.

If the user moves an element from one document to another, we may have to do two things:

- Change the element's document to the new one.

- Change the element's location in the new document.

We made two changes, but the user expects the undo operation to cancel both of them.

Creating an undo group is easy:

```
context.undoManager?.beginUndoGrouping()
// make the changes
context.undoManager?.endUndoGrouping()
```

We need to make sure that once we begin a group, we also end it.

Generally speaking, the undo feature is probably not something you are going to use every day – it's related to the type of app you are working at and in a specific use case.

But first, it shows how nicely Apple engineers took an old library and integrated it into the NSManagedObjectContext.

And second, when you do need it, it's very powerful and convenient, so it's good to have it in your arsenal as an iOS developer.

Summary

This chapter was just the tip of the ice of how to implement Core Data in your apps – there is so much more.

But the goal was to give you an overview of how it works in the real world.

We've learned about separations, handling network requests, observing data changes, `NSFetchedResultsController,` and the UndoManager.

In the next chapter, we will dive even deeper and talk about concurrency and how it fits with reactive programming.

CHAPTER 8

Concurrency and Declarative Programming

The way the processor industry is going, is to add more and more cores, but nobody knows how to program those things. I mean, two, yeah; four, not really; eight, forget it.

—Steve Jobs

For some reason, **concurrency** in Core Data sounds scary for many developers, primarily because of crashes and lagging.

The truth is that concurrency in Core Data is pretty simple, as long as we keep some basic rules.

After all, reading this book to this point proves that I am dealing here with a pretty intelligent developer.

Despite its advantages, another related issue that scares many developers is to move to **declarative programming**.

In this chapter, we are going to "face our fears" and learn how concurrency and declarative programming work and how to combine them together.

© Avi Tsadok 2022
A. Tsadok, *Unleash Core Data*, https://doi.org/10.1007/978-1-4842-8211-3_8

We are going to learn about

- The different rules regarding concurrency

- What exactly are private contexts and how to create them

- How to perform actions using these contexts

- The different concurrency patterns and how to choose the right one for your needs

- How SwiftUI and Core Data go together

- How to import data from the Web using Combine

These Rules Are Written in Blood

Well, maybe not actually blood, more like long nights of tired developers trying to figure out why their code keeps crashing.

There are some basic rules that should protect your app from crashes and lags, so pay attention carefully!

Contexts Are Not Thread-Safe

The first rule: Each thread has its own managed object context. Remember we talked about contexts and I mentioned something called a "private" context?

Well, now is the time to reveal what private context means.

For background operations, we will use **private context** and, for UI thread operations, **main contexts**.

Don't perform operations on contexts outside their thread! We will see examples of how to make sure this is not happening.

Managed Objects Belong to Their Context Thread

This is critical – managed objects live on their context's thread. Moving objects between contexts may cause your app to crash!

There are several ways to handle that, such as passing references like ManagedObjectID (I'll show you an example), a struct (which is thread-safe), and even using the external object ID (e.g., "songID") and then reloading it on the new thread.

There are several ways. What's more important for you is to use them.

Writing in Private Context, Reading in Main Context

Even though Core Data is very efficient, heavy load tasks should happen in the background.

We are going to see different strategies of how to handle various tasks for different use cases, but the basic working assumption is that **writing should happen on a private thread and fetching on the main thread**.

The "separation of concerns" principle (my favorite one) is applied here as well – every context needs to have its own goal.

Now let's go find out what's that thing called "private contexts."

Private Contexts

I know we've already discussed contexts in one of our chapters, but now is the time to discuss ever deeper.

Private contexts are aimed to address background operations. Trying to work with private contexts on the main thread will raise an exception. (Remember that's one of the rules? If not, go back and reread them.)

Creating

We have two ways to create a private context.

First, we can create a private context just like we create a main context –initialize it and pass the .privateQueueConcurrencyType type:

```
privateContext = NSManagedObjectContext(concurrencyType:
.privateQueueConcurrencyType)
```

And now, we need to connect the context to our Core Data stack somehow. Otherwise, it's just "out of context" (got it?).

So we can either connect it to a persistent store coordinator, like this:

```
privateContext.persistentStoreCoordinator =
persistentContainer.persistentStoreCoordinator
```

Or provide it with a parent context, which can be either main or private (depends on our strategy):

```
privateContext.parent = mainContext
```

The other option that we have to create a private context is to use a dedicated container method named newBackgroundContext():

```
privateContext = persistentContainer.newBackgroundContext()
```

The newBackgroundContext() returns a new (private) context that is already connected to the persistent store coordinator.

Performing Actions

Okay, now that we have a private context, let's try to perform some actions in the context safely.

In general, if the context is private, you cannot know what thread it belongs to.

The best way to make sure we are executing actions on the right thread is to use the perform() method:

```
privateContext.perform { [unowned self] in
            let newSong = Song(context: self.
            privateContext)
        do {
            try self.privateContext.save()
        } catch let error {
            // handle error
        }

    }
```

The perform() method makes the executed code in the closure run on the correct private context thread.

One thing to notice here: Calling the perform method also makes sure the code runs asynchronously .

This means that if we run the following code, "2" will be printed first:

```
privateContext.perform { [unowned self] in
            // some context work
            print("1")
    }
    print("2") // this will be printed first.
    updateUI()
```

If we expect to update the UI at the end of the closure, using perform() can be a problem. After the runner calls the perform() method, it continues to the following line without waiting for the closure work to finish.

That is why the code will print the "2" and then "1".

performAndWait()

If we want to sync our operations, we need to use a different method –
performAndWait:

```
privateContext.performAndWait { [unowned self] in
            let newSong = Song(context: self.
            privateContext)
        do {
            try self.privateContext.save()
            print("1") // this will be printed first
        } catch let error {

        }
    }

print("2") // this will printed second
updateUI()
```

In this case, "1" will be printed first, followed by "2".

You probably scratch your head and think about why it matters,
but once we talk about the different strategies to handle concurrency,
everything will be more straightforward.

performBackgroundTask()

Another convenient method we can use is performBackgroundTask().

Unlike the perform and peformAndWait methods that belong
to contexts, performBackgroundTask is a method that belongs to
NSPersistentContainer:

```
delegate.persistentContainer.performBackgroundTask {
privateContext in
            let newSong = Song(context: privateContext)
    }
```

Whenever we call performBackgroundTask, the container creates a **new private context** for us and executes the closure code on the correct thread.

The context created in performBackgroundTask is connected to the container persistent store, and calling save() will push the changes directly to the store.

Concurrency Patterns

performBackgroundTask looks like a convenient tool, doesn't it?

We just call it, a new context is being created on the spot, and we can forget about it a minute later.

Not so fast!

Creating a temporary context for making some modifications in the background is **not a strategy**. It is perfectly fine to do that, but beyond the convenience that it brings, you need to think about the consequences.

But what could be the consequences? The main problem with performBackgroundTask is that the container creates a new context **every time you call it** and then performs an async operation.

Look at the following method:

```
func updateSongName(songID: String, newName: String) {
    persistentContainer.performBackgroundTask {
    privateContext in
        let fetchRequest = NSFetchRequest<Song>(entityNa
        me: "Song")
        fetchReuqest.predicate = NSPredicate(format:
        "songID = %@", songID)
        do {
            let song = try privateContext.
            fetch(fetchRequest).first
```

```
            song?.name = newName
            try privateContext.save()
        } catch let error {
            print(error.localizedDescription)
        }
    }
}
```

The function opens a temporary private context, fetches a song by its ID, updates its name, and pushes the changes to the context.

Now, let's think - what happens if we call that function twice from two different places?

The answer: Two contexts will be created, which are not synced with each other, and we can have a race condition with an unexpected result! But that's expected because that's the nature of concurrency work.

Now, I gave a basic example just to prove my point, but you should think more prominent than that– these problems can occur in sync from the server combining with user actions or with multiple actions on the same screen.

What should we do? We need to have a strategy that will make sure our actions are synced with the persistent store and the UI and even with each other.

So let's talk about different patterns to handle our actions correctly.

Parent/Child Strategy

The parent/child strategy is probably the simplest one. This strategy is built upon several assumptions:

- The view context is the **only context** connected to the persistent store.

- Private contexts have the view context or another private context as their parent.

- Write operations are done in **private contexts only**.

- It is best practice to create private contexts for specific flows.

Let's see what the relationships between the different components look like (Figure 8-1).

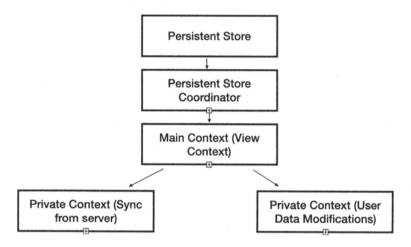

Figure 8-1. *Parent/child strategy*

And now for the code itself:

```
class CoreDataStack {

let viewContext : NSManagedObjectContext {
        (UIApplication.shared.delegate as! AppDelegate).
        persistentContainer.viewContext
    }

var syncPrivateContext: NSManagedObjectContext!
Var userPrivateContext: NSManagedObjectContext!
Static let shared = CoreDataStack()

init() {
```

```
    syncPrivateContext = NSManagedObjectContext(concurrency
    Type: .privateQueueConcurrencyType)
    syncPrivateContext.parent = viewContext

    userPrivateContext = NSManagedObjectContext(concurrency
    Type: .privateQueueConcurrencyType)
    userPrivateContext.parent = viewContext
  }
}
```

Read the code carefully, and you'll see how simple it is – I created two private contexts and set the main context as their parent.

So how do we actually make changes to our store?

Remember that to save data in a context, we push the changes to its parent (if it exists) and to the persistent store (if set).

So in our example, calling save() in one of the private contexts pushes the changes to the main context.

After the main context is updated, we can call save() in the main context to push the changes to the persistent store.

The following function inserts a new song to the persistent store while doing that in the background:

```
func insertNewSong(withName name: String) {
    CoreDataStack.shared.userPrivateContext.perform {
        let song = Song(context: CoreDataStack.shared.
        userPrivateContext)
        song.name = name

        do {
            try CoreDataStack.shared.
            userPrivateContext.save()

            CoreDataStack.shared.viewContext.
            performAndWait {
```

```
do {
    try CoreDataStack.shared.
    viewContext.save()
} catch let error {
    print("Error pushing changes to
    the persistent store - %@", error.
    localizedDescription)
    }
  }
} catch let error {
    NSLog("Error pushing changes to the main
    context- %@", error.localizedDescription)
    }
  }
}
```

The function does exactly what we've talked about. Notice the usage of the perform() and performAndWait().

We started by calling perform() in the private context because we didn't want to block the UI.

Inside the thread itself, we called performAndWait() because we wanted the actions to be synced when we were inside a thread.

Private in Front

The child/parent pattern is simple to understand – we have a view context connected to the persistent store and one or more private child contexts for heavy load operations.

A different approach we can take is to reverse the way our stack is built.

Instead of connecting the view context to the persistent store coordinator, we will connect the private context instead, and it will be our parent context (Figure 8-2).

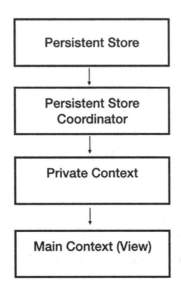

Figure 8-2. *Private context as parent*

Let's see how we build it in code step by step.

I'll start with the private context. Remember it's the parent context now:

```
private lazy var privateContext: NSManagedObjectContext = {
    var managedObjectContext = NSManagedObjectContext(concu
    rrencyType: .privateQueueConcurrencyType)
    managedObjectContext.persistentStoreCoordinator = self.
    persistentStoreCoordinator
    return managedObjectContext
}()
```

You can see I created a lazy-loading variable and connected it to the persistent store directly.

And now for the view context:

```
private lazy var viewContext: NSManagedObjectContext = {
    let managedObjectContext = NSManagedObjectContext(concu
    rrencyType: .mainQueueConcurrencyType)
```

```
    managedObjectContext.parent = self.privateContext
    return managedObjectContext
}()
```

The view context is not connected to the persistent store, but to the parent context we saw earlier.

Now, what is the benefit of that pattern?

In a way, it simplifies our Core Data usage.

Because the main context pushes its changes to the private context (which is its parent) and the private context saves the new data on a background thread, it means that the rest of the app always works with one context only – the view context.

We don't need to think whether we are writing or reading.

Let's see a save operation in practice:

```
func saveChanges() {
    mainContext.perform {
        do {
            if self.mainContext.hasChanges {
                try self.mainContext.save()
            }
        } catch {
            let saveError = error as Error
            print("\(saveError), \(saveError.
            localizedDescription)")
        }

        self.privateContext.perform {
            do {
                if self.privateContext.hasChanges {
                    try self.privateContext.save()
                }
```

```
        } catch {
            let saveError = error as Error
            print("\(saveError), \(saveError.
            localizedDescription)")
        }
    }
  }
}
```

As I said earlier, we first push the changes to the private context and then save them in the persistent store.

From the point of view of the UI, it just needs to call the save method.

What to Choose?

Let me clear things up before we continue.

The strategies I just presented are not set in stone, and there are probably more strategies out there.

I brought them here mainly to give you a sense of **how concurrency works** in practice and the essential tools to implement some of it in your apps.

And still, we need to define what direction to take.

To do that, there are some things we need to consider and questions we need to ask ourselves:

- Do we have any **long and heavy data operations** such as sync or data import?

- Is our app mostly based on **quick data changes** because of user actions?

- Do we need to create child contexts to allow the user to **edit an object** and dismiss it if needed?

Parent/child strategies are mostly for apps with **heavy tasks** that we wish to do in the background. That strategy makes it easy to create private contexts for specific purposes and lets them work in the background.

On the other side, the "Private in Front" strategy pushes **small changes and updates** to the persistent store while keeping your UI working with one context only (doing all the work from the UI perspective).

Do you see how much not scary concurrency is?

Hopefully, you have the tools now to decide what best fits your app.

Declarative Programming

There is a direct link between concurrency discussions and declarative programming.

The problem with many Core Data books and articles is that it is elementary and comfortable to talk about the app's data layer and forget that there's a UI that needs to be constantly updated.

And it's not only the UI layer – complex apps have complex architectures, with multiple layers that are supposed to communicate with each other.

And what do you know? We are about to exit our comfort zone and investigate that area!

First, what exactly is **declarative programming**?

In imperative programming patterns, the data flows are handled like this:

- The user taps on a button.

- The button modifies our data.

- We update the UI according to the new data.

We can see that the preceding steps work. Kind of.

I can point out several issues with it:

- There're maybe **additional cases** where the data can be changed other than pressing a button, so we need to handle these cases as well (even if we already moved on from developing that screen – we then need to go back and handle that use case).

- The data that was changed because of the button tapping **may affect more views**, so it's something we need to handle as well.

In declarative programming, the UI is **derived from our data**. We declare how the UI components look based on data, and when we change the data, the UI updates itself automatically and efficiently.

One thing to notice: When I'm talking about Core Data and declarative programming, **I'm not referring only to UI**. Declarative programming can also be in other layers of the app.

Even though the concept is not new, in this book, I will demonstrate how declarative programming and Core Data work together using the relatively new Combine framework.

I will do that using some code examples and tricks that you can build upon.

And don't worry – we will talk about communication not only between the persistent store and the UI but also in other places of the app.

Note   To understand the following several pages, you need to have a basic knowledge of the Combine framework. If you don't know what Combine is, stop here and search the Web for some tutorials and examples before continuing.

SwiftUI and Core Data

Apple presented the SwiftUI framework during WWDC19 along with iOS 13.

SwiftUI is the "new and slick way of building UI" based on the Combine framework to update its state.

Apple really redesigned some of the developing methods we used in the past and even made changes in Core Data to support them, for example, the `NSManagedObject` class.

Managed Object Support

SwiftUI state can be based on something called `ObservableObject`. `ObservableObject` is a protocol with a publisher that emits before the object has changed.

Now, here's a secret many iOS developers don't know – `NSManagedObject` conforms to the `ObservableObject` protocol out of the box!

So binding a managed object to a SwiftUI view just works:

```swift
struct Screen: View {

    @ObservedObject var song: Song

    var body: some View {
        VStack {
            Text(song.name!)
        }
    }
}
```

You remember that `Song` is a managed object, right?

So, if the song name property changes, the UI will be updated automatically.

By the way, you don't need SwiftUI to enjoy that feature. Here's a UIKit example:

```
@Published var song: Song!
var anyCancellables = Set<AnyCancellable>()

override func viewDidLoad() {
    super.viewDidLoad()

    $song.sink {[weak unowned] song in
        self.myLabel.text = song?.name ?? ""
    }.store(in: &anyCancellables)
```

See? You don't need to move to SwiftUI to use Combine with Core Data.

Now let's see the SwiftUI version of NSFetchedResultsController.

@FetchRequest

The combination of SwiftUI and Combine really simplifies how our UI responds to the changes.

If that reminds you of something we've learned in the previous chapter, you are not wrong – I'm talking about NSFetchedResultsController.

Apple took a step forward and created a property wrapper called @FetchRequest, which works quite similar to what we know from NSFetchedResultsController, but with much less code.

The way we declare a @FetchRequest property wrapper is simple:

```
@FetchRequest(entity: Song.entity(),
              sortDescriptors: [
    NSSortDescriptor(keyPath: \Song.name, ascending: true)
    ],
    predicate: NSPredicate(format: "isFavorite = %@", true)
) var songs: FetchedResults<Song>
```

In the preceding example, the @FetchRequest property takes three parameters – the entity we are fetching, an array of sort descriptors, and a predicate. The results of the fetch request are stored in a variable named songs.

At this point, you don't need to do anything. Just connect the songs variable to the UI (here's the full code):

```
struct SongList: View {
    @FetchRequest(entity: Song.entity(),
                sortDescriptors: [
        NSSortDescriptor(keyPath: \Song.name, ascending: true)
        ],
        predicate: NSPredicate(format: "isFavorite = %@", true)
    ) var songs: FetchedResults<Song>

    var body: some View {
        List(songs, id: \.id) { song in
                SongRow(song: song)
        }.environment(\.managedObjectContext, CoreDataStack.
        shared.viewContext)
    }
}
```

We can learn two more things from the preceding example. First, the songs variable **automatically reloads** whenever there is a change in the fetch results.

Second, we need to pass the **relevant context** as an environment to the view.

Where Did My View Model Go?

The main problem with the examples I just showed you is the ignoring of what most developers use as their primary design pattern – the **view model**.

One of the rules we need to enforce when using the @FetchRequest property wrapper is that it must be in the view itself, which is kind of missing the point of MVVM.

If we want to have good separations of our app, it is better to have layers because each has a different responsibility and role. Look at Figure 8-3.

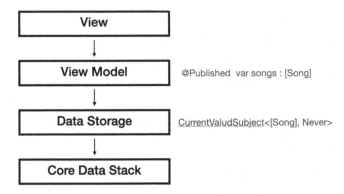

Figure 8-3. *Core Data with MVVM*

Of course, your app architecture doesn't have to look like Figure 8-3, as it can have additional layers like business logic or more services. But the point is clear – layers should only "know" stuff under their responsibility.

So what is the "Data Storage" component?

The Data Storage component holds managed objects relevant to a screen or a feature and is getting updated using an NSFetchedResultsController.

Our architecture looks like this:

- The **Data Storage** component gets updates from the Core Data stack using an FRC and has a CurrentValueSubject publisher that holds the updated items and publishes changes.

- The **View Model** gets updates from the data storage and has a @Published variable so it can publish changes to the view.

- The **View** reloads itself by listening to the view model.

Let's look at some code. Here is the data storage class:

```
class SongsScreenStorage: NSObject {
    var songs = CurrentValueSubject<[Song], Never>([])
    private var frc : NSFetchedResultsController<Song>

    override init() {
        frc = NSFetchedResultsController(fetchRequest: Song.
        fetchRequest(), managedObjectContext: CoreDataStack.
        shared.mainContext, sectionNameKeyPath: nil,
        cacheName: nil)
        super.init()
        frc.delegate = self
        do {
            try frc.performFetch()
        } catch {
            NSLog("Oops, could not fetch songs")
        }
    }
}

extension SongsScreenStorage:
NSFetchedResultsControllerDelegate {
    func controllerDidChangeContent(_ controller: NSFetchedResu
    ltsController<NSFetchRequestResult>) {
        guard let songs = controller.fetchedObjects as?
        [Song] else {
            return
```

```
    }
    self.songs.value = songs
  }
}
```

As I said earlier, the data storage is built upon an
NSFetchedResultsController and implements only one delegate method
to update the CurrentValueSubject publisher.

What's left for the view model is to **observe any changes** we have in
the songs list:

```
class SongsScreenViewModel: ObservableObject {

    @Published var songs: [Song] = []
    private var cancellable = Set<AnyCancellable>()
    var dataStorage = SongsScreenStorage()

    init() {
        dataStorage.songs.sink { songs in
            self.songs = songs
        }.store(in: &cancellable)
    }
}
```

You should be aware that everything I presented here is just a
suggestion. You can manipulate the architecture and the design patterns
any way you want. Here are some examples:

- We can make the **data storage a Singleton** and share it
  with multiple view models and views.

- We can **initialize the data storage with a predicate**
  and make it more reusable.

- We can create one Singleton that holds **several data
  storage instances** for each model.

Also, notice that the preceding architecture has nothing to do with SwiftUI – we can implement it in UIKit as well, and that's another advantage – now it's easy to replace the view with a view controller.

Import Data from the Web to Core Data

Another common use case where Combine and Core Data go together is importing data from a server and saving it locally.

Remember it is a best practice to insert objects using a background thread and avoid performance issues.

What we are going to do here is to extend the DTO that we received from the server and add an insertToCoreData() method that returns a publisher:

```
extension ImportedSongDTO {

    func insertToCoreData() -> Future<NSManagedObjectID,
    Error> {
        return Future() { promise in
            let context = CoreDataStack.shared.privateContext
            context.perform {
                do {
                    let newSong = Song(context: context)
                    newSong.name = self.name
                    try context.save()
                    promise(.success(newSong.objectID))
                } catch {
                    promise(Result.failure(error))
                }
            }
        }
    }
}
```

Here are a few things to notice:

- We took the private context we have in the
  CoreDataStack and called its perform function.

- We return a publisher with an NSManagedObjectID
  value instead of NSManagedObject. Can you think why?
  The simple answer is that we don't want to pass an
  NSManagedObject to another thread. Remember that
  NSManagedObject is not thread-safe. The only way to
  load the same managed object on a different thread is
  to give its NSManagedObjectID and then load it again.

- We are taking advantage of the built-in support of
  Combine with throwing errors and returning the Error
  we get inside the Future closure.

Now, to connect the importToCoreData() function to the URL, we just
need to chain it:

```swift
func importSongFromNetwork() {
        let url = URL(string: "https://www.mywebsite.com/api")!

        URLSession.shared.dataTaskPublisher(for: url)
            .tryMap{ data, response -> Data in
                return data
            }.decode(type: ImportedSongDTO.self, decoder:
            JSONDecoder())
            .flatMap { importedSong in
                return importedSong.insertToCoreData()
            }
            .eraseToAnyPublisher()
            .sink { completion in

            } receiveValue: { objectIDInserted in
```

```
    }.store(in: &cancellables)
}
```

Note   Again, remember that the examples I show you are just suggestions. You can improve and adjust them to your needs.

In general, extending your DTOs with publishers is always a good idea to improve your code readability and handle concurrency work.

Summary

This was an advanced chapter that showed you how concurrency is handled in Core Data, especially around contexts.

Also, we saw how we could take that concurrency work to the next level by implementing reactive programing.

I have a feeling that now is the point that you need to feel more comfortable with Core Data in general. We did some neat things in this chapter!

And speaking of "neat things," in the next chapter, we will learn how we can optimize Core Data for performance.

CHAPTER 9

Performance

*Start by doing what's necessary, then what's possible, and
suddenly you are doing the impossible.*

—Francis of Assisi

How to make a speedy framework even faster?

The main thing we need to do is understand how it works and combine
the result with our needs.

And this is what this chapter is all about.

In this chapter, we are going to talk about

- – Faulting and how to take advantage of it

- – How to improve our fetches using a fetch index

- – How to improve our string search

- – How to improve our saving operations

- – Profiling our app using Instruments

Faulting

In one of my Core Data examples in this book, I showed you the
following code:

```
let albumName = song.album.name
```

© Avi Tsadok 2022
A. Tsadok, *Unleash Core Data*, https://doi.org/10.1007/978-1-4842-8211-3_9

That short line of code shows that once I fetched a song, it was super simple to get its album name.

But wait – have you ever wondered **how it is possible**?

All you need to do is access the song's album name property. Does this mean that we also brought its album when we fetched the song object?

And what happens in the next line of code?

```
let otherAlbumSongs = song.album.songs
```

You must admit this is strange – even if fetching a song also fetches its album, fetching the other album's songs is too much!

I ask you, Where does it end?

First, don't worry. Look at the following code – I fetched the albums I have in the persistent store, printed them to the console, and got this:

```
<Album: 0x600002c0b520> (entity: Album; id: 0xd3a324599d489ce4
<x-coredata://1D3024C7-8EFC-4A8E-879C-FE019FDF5E91/Album/p1>;
data: <fault>)
```

You probably know that there are cases where we print Core Data objects and get their properties' values.

For some reason, that's not the case in the preceding example. Instead of getting the full object details, we get some general information, and under data, we get fault (marked in bold).

So what does "fault" means?

"Faulting" is one of Core Data's best features and what makes it so efficient on the one hand but so convenient on the other.

Faulting means that Core Data does not go to the persistent store to query data unless it really needs to, and instead, it keeps a hashable representation of the object in memory.

The fact that we lazy-load our data has a huge (positive) impact on performance and memory.

Let's see how faulting works step by step:

```
let fetchRequest = Album.fetchRequest()
let myAlbum = try context.fetch(fetchRequest).first
```

myAlbum is a fault now – this means that its actual data are not fetched yet.

Now, we want to get the album title:

```
let title = myAlbum?.title
```

At this point, Core Data goes to the persistent store and fetches the album details. Now, if we print the album object, we'll see its full details:

```
▽ Optional<Album>
  - some : <Album: 0x6000033a6c10> (entity: Album; id:
  0xae68e3f8a8d01a17 <x-coredata://1D3024C7-8EFC-4A8E-879C-
  FE019FDF5E91/Album/p1>; data: {
    id = nil;
    num = 5;
    releaseDate = nil;
    songs = "<relationship fault: 0x6000010c4280 'songs'>";
    title = "Dark Side of The Moon";
})
```

Notice that now, the songs' relationship is a fault. That's because we didn't ask for any information about the songs themselves. Only if we access the songs object Core Data will query the persistent store and get their data.

Amazing and clever as it is, **where does it meet us** as developers?

So the way faulting works is transparent to us. We basically don't need to do anything for it to work, and that's one of Core Data beauties.

But understating how it works can help us solve performance issues and even make our code even more efficient.

Batch Faulting

Let's get back to our previous example with fetching an album and its songs.

What we want to do now is getting all the album songs:

```
if let songs = myAlbum?.songs?.allObjects as? [Song] {
    let names = songs.map{$0.name}
}
```

Simple, right?

If we turn on the Core Data debugging (adding -com.apple.CoreData. SQLDebug 1 in the scheme arguments), we are going to see the following:

```
SELECT 0, to.Z_PK, to.Z_OPT, to.ZDURATION, to.ZIMAGEURL,
to.ZNAME, to.ZNUMBER, to.ZALBUM, to.ZCOMPOSER, to.ZLYRICS FROM
ZSONG to WHERE  to.Z_PK = ?
```

For every song in the array

If we have 100 songs, we will query the store 100 times.

If we have a very long array, Core Data will do many roundtrips to the persistent store, of course, in the name of faulting.

So the Core Data faulting feature is smart but not that smart.

This is where we can help Core Data faulting be more efficient, and we can do that using something called "**batch faulting**."

If we want to fault a big array of objects at once, we can do the following:

```
if let songs = myAlbum?.songs?.allObjects as? [Song] {
    let predicate = NSPredicate(format: "SELF in %@", songs)
    let fetchRequest = Song.fetchRequest()
    fetchRequest.predicate = predicate
    fetchRequest.returnsObjectsAsFaults = false
    let fullSongsData = try context.fetch(fetchRequest)
}
```

I want to explain what the code does.

After we have all the album songs in an array, we create a fetch request that re-fetch the same songs list, in some "predicate trick":

```
let predicate = NSPredicate(format: "SELF in %@", songs)
```

We can define that the fetch request won't return the results as faulted objects by setting the `returnsObjectsAsFaults` property as false.

As always, we need to understand the prices and consequences of what we are doing.

Faulting is not there because some computer science students had to do a college assignment.

Faulting helps you reduce memory footprint. It means that loading all the songs into the memory impacts your app.

Let's say you have 1000 items you want to display in a UITableView. Fetching all their content to the memory will be a huge mistake – the user probably won't scroll the bottom of the table view anyway, so there's no point in consuming so much memory.

But in the case of mapping like the preceding example, batch faulting can be a good solution.

Always balance between memory and speed, and that's also the case here.

Prefetching

Another way to fetch data efficiently is something called **prefetching**.

Going back to the previous example, when we fetched the album object, we also said, "I want to fetch its songs as well."

Well, this is something we can simply define in our fetch request, by providing a key path:

```
let fetchRequest = Album.fetchRequest()           fetchRequest
.relationshipKeyPathsForPrefetching = ["songs"]
let myAlbum = try context.fetch(fetchRequest).first
```

Providing a list of key paths and setting them in the relationshipKeyPathsForPrefetching will also fetch them.

Looking at the console, we can see Core Data performs two queries. The first query gets the album details:

```
SELECT 0, t0.Z_PK, t0.Z_OPT, t0.ZID, t0.ZNUM, t0.ZRELEASEDATE,
t0.ZTITLE FROM ZALBUM t0
```

The second query fetches the details of the songs:

```
SELECT 0, t0.Z_PK, t0.Z_OPT, t0.ZDURATION, t0.ZIMAGEURL,
t0.ZNAME, t0.ZNUMBER, t0.ZALBUM, t0.ZCOMPOSER, t0.ZLYRICS
FROM ZSONG t0 WHERE  t0.ZALBUM IN (SELECT * FROM _Z_
intarray0)  ORDER BY t0.ZALBUM
```

Even though it's not always clear what the column names mean, it's easy to understand what the query is supposed to do – I marked in bold the expressions that can lead to what it's doing.

Like batch faulting, we interfere with how Core Data optimizes its work. You should balance between memory and speed here and understand its impact.

Deleting

"But you said we don't need to do anything!"

And you don't!

In this topic, you just need to lean back and read because it's for your knowledge self-enrichment only.

Now, a question: We fetch an album, and its songs are a fault. We delete one of the songs from the persistent store in another context. What will happen if the first context tries to fire (meaning load data for a faulted item) the deleted song?

Before iOS 9, the app would crash, and you got this error:

```
Terminating app due to uncaught exception
'NSObjectInaccessibleException', reason: 'CoreData could not
fulfill a fault for
```

The preceding case is one of the reasons Core Data frustrated so many developers over the years.

As I said, iOS 9 changed that, and now if a faulted item is being deleted in the persistent store, it is also being removed from the other contexts.

If you want to experience how developers felt before iOS 9, you can restore that behavior by configuring your context:

```
context.shouldDeleteInaccessibleFaults = false
```

Setting the shouldDeleteInaccessibleFaults property to false makes sure your app will crash when accessing deleted faulted objects.

Isn't it lovely? (See, I said you just need to lean back and read.)

Improve Your Fetches

We already know that Core Data is super-efficient and fast. Core Data fetches are extremely fast, partly because of the reasons we've discussed earlier.

How fast?

I built a small app with a persistent store that contains around 100,000 songs.

I ran a fetch request with the following predicate:

```
let predicate = NSPredicate(format: "name = %@", "Don't Stop
Me Now")
```

The execution time was 0.0357 seconds. Insanely fast!

Even though it was on my MacBook Pro M1, it is impressive.

But we can make it even faster by using a fetch index.

Fetch Index

A fetch index is one of the Core Data APIs that can help us specify an index for specific attributes in our store.

So what's an index?

For those who are not familiar with how classic databases are optimized, an index is another table that helps queries avoid what we call a "full table scan."

The best way to explain that is by using the book you are just holding. If you want to jump to a specific chapter or locate a particular term, you don't need to go page by page from the start.

We know why – we have a menu or an index for that.

The same goes with tables. If we want to have an efficient query, we need to **create an index** for specific columns.

Back to Core Data. Underneath this great framework, we have a database with the same rules of full table scan as well.

To understand how the fetch request I mentioned earlier performed, we will first enable our Core Data SQL debugging in our scheme editor.

Go to Product ➤ Scheme ➤ Edit Scheme.

There, go to the Run action and, under Arguments, add the following:

```
-com.apple.CoreData.SQLDebug 4
```

This time, we are setting the debug level to 4 instead of 1 to get more information about our Core Data activity.

Look at Figure 9-1 for help.

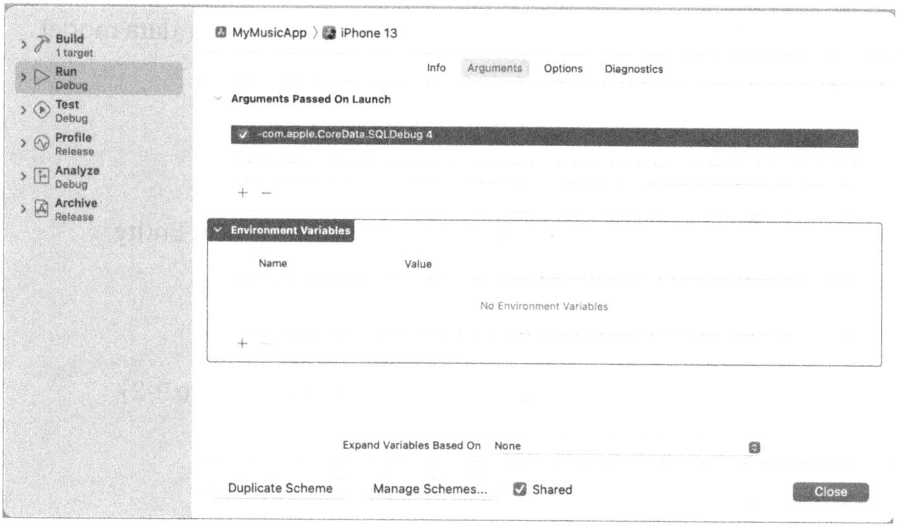

Figure 9-1. *Enable Core Data debugging, level 4*

Now, when we rerun the app, we are going to see interesting information in our console, and especially this EXPLAIN statement:

```
CoreData: details: SQLite: EXPLAIN QUERY PLAN SELECT 0, to.Z_
PK, to.Z_OPT, to.ZDURATION, to.ZIMAGEURL, to.ZNAME, to.ZNUMBER,
to.ZALBUM, to.ZCOMPOSER, to.ZLYRICS FROM ZSONG to WHERE  to.
ZNAME = ? LIMIT 1
     3 0 0 SCAN to
```

The SCAN word you see in bold means that SQLite had to perform a full table scan in the Songs ("ZSONG") table.

So, even though the performance was good, a full table scan is something we want to avoid using a fetch index.

Creating a Fetch Index

Creating a fetch index is very simple and easily done in your data model editor (remember that window?):

- Open your data model editor and select your Song entity.

- Select Editor ➤ Add Fetch Index, or click the Add Entity button in the bottom.

- Select Add Fetch Index.

- A new fetch index is created for you (look at Figure 9-2).

Figure 9-2. *A new fetch index*

We will give our new fetch index a name, in this case – byName.

We will add a new fetch index element on the right by clicking the plus button and selecting the name property.

Now, we should see something like Figure 9-3.

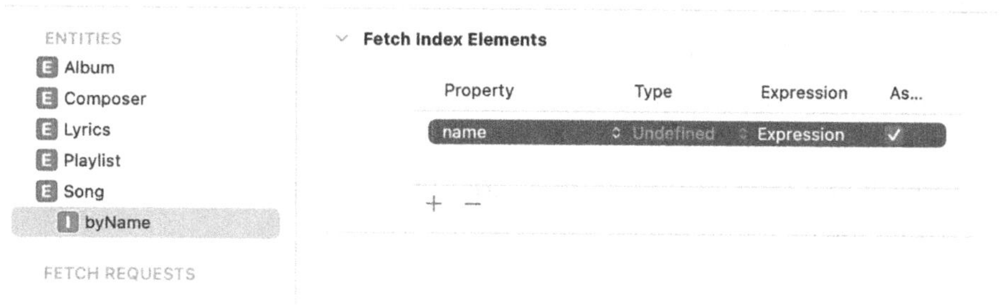

Figure 9-3. *A new fetch index element based on the name property*

Now, let's rerun the same request and see how it performs:

```
CoreData: annotation: total fetch execution time: 0.0357s
for 1 rows.
```

Same duration as the previous fetch?

"But you promised!"

I know I did. But indexing is not "magic." It is another table Core Data needs to build if it wants to use it.

We've got several ways to make the table build happen:

- Reinstalling the app

- Creating a model version (we'll talk about it in the next chapter)

- Changing the entity hash modifier.

Now for the explanation.

When Core Data loads the persistent store, it compares the data model scheme defined in the app with the current scheme the store is based on.

If Core Data finds differences, it starts something called migration.

Even though we will learn about migration later in that book, you should be aware that migration triggers the building of an index.

Defining a fetch index is not a scheme change. Therefore, **it doesn't trigger** migration.

So one way to trigger migration is to create a model version that is different from the previous one.

Another way to trigger migration is to **provide a different Hash Modifier** with all the entities we want to build their index.

To change to a different hash modifier

– Go to the data model editor.

– Select the entity whose hash modifier you want to change.

– Select the inspector pane on the right.

– Locate the hash modifier at the bottom.

You can look at Figure 9-4.

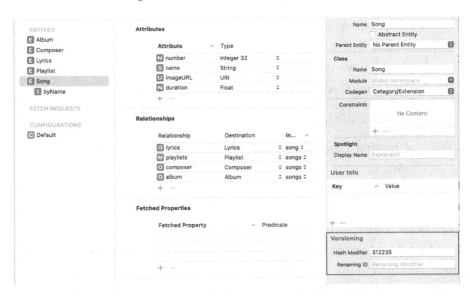

Figure 9-4. *Changing the hash modifier*

All you need to do is to pick a different hash modifier. The simple way is increasing its number.

Rerunning the app with the new hash modifier and the fetch index will print the following message to the console (as long our Core Data debugging is enabled), which indicates the index build works:

```
CREATE INDEX IF NOT EXISTS Z_Song_byName ON ZSONG (ZNAME
COLLATE BINARY ASC)
```

We can also see from the EXPLAIN statement in the console that now, querying for songs doesn't perform a full table scan but instead uses the index we've just created:

```
details: SQLite: EXPLAIN QUERY PLAN SELECT 0, t0.Z_PK,
t0.Z_OPT, t0.ZDURATION, t0.ZIMAGEURL, t0.ZNAME, t0.ZNUMBER,
t0.ZALBUM, t0.ZCOMPOSER, t0.ZLYRICS FROM ZSONG t0 WHERE
t0.ZNAME = ? LIMIT 1
    4 0 0 SEARCH t0 USING INDEX Z_Song_byName (ZNAME=?)
```

And how is the performance?

```
CoreData: annotation: total fetch execution time: 0.0065s
for 1 rows
```

Much better than before!

Note   The duration of the fetch requests I mentioned here is not important – they were done on my laptop using a simulator. What's important is to see the change the fetch index made to my request. You can expect different results on another machine, but the improvement stays.

Index Expressions

You and I know that predicates are more complicated than just comparing strings.

If we go back to Chapter 5, I showed you we could also fetch data using expressions.

For example, this is the usage of a sum function:

```
let sumDurationExpression = NSExpression(forFunction: "sum:",
arguments: [keyPathExpression])
```

The preceding expression can be implemented in a fetch request using NSExpressionDescription (go over Chapter 6 again).

If expressions are something you perform with a large set of objects, you can index them as well!

Going back to the data model, instead of choosing an attribute to index, you can choose an expression (Figure 9-5).

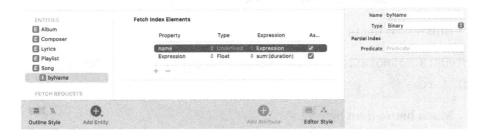

Figure 9-5. *Creating a fetch index element for an expression*

Now performing a sum operation on song duration has never been faster!

Indexing expressions really nails it – it's one of the cases where optimizations are being served to you and you just need to take them.

Is a Fetch Index a Magic?

What you're asking is, If a fetch index works so well, why not create a fetch index for all entities and attributes? What do we have to lose?

(I don't know if that's what you asked, but let's pretend that's what happened.)

So not only a fetch index can be handy; sometimes it's a must. Doing a full table scan on large data sets is considered bad practice.

But on the other hand, the fetch index is not magic.

Indexes have their cost.

Let's restore the "book example" again.

We have an index for fast locating of terms and subjects in our book.

We notice that the index consumes extra pages of the book, which translates to disk space in the computer world.

But space is the least of our problems.

What happens when we edit, delete, or add more pages to our book?

Now that we have an index, we need to maintain it as well!

So we now understand that an index requires not only space but **also time**.

Having too many indexes can harm your app performance, and ironically that was something you wanted to improve!

Believe it or not, there are times when adding indexes might create an overload on your app, so be careful and always check the impact of your actions on different metrics.

Use One-to-One Relationships to Improve Performance

Wait...what?

How does using relationships relate to performance?

When we talked about relationships, we mentioned the form of a one-to-one relationship, which can be an extension of an object.

If you think intuitively, having entities with many attributes hurts both your memory and your fetch time.

One option to avoid that is using the Core Data's faulting feature, which lazy-loads additional data.

Take the Album entity as an example.

If we want to extend the Album entity with information about the releasing process, for example, who was the musical producer, where it was released, and even pictures, we can add it as part of the Album with more attributes.

But adding more attributes to the Album may impact its loading time when we have a significant amount of data.

A solution might be to create another entity named `AlbumRelasingDetails` and connect it to Album as a one-to-one relationship.

It's a great way to load only what you need, and it's also a great example of how much the separation of concerns principle is helpful in our code.

Limit Your Results

That tip is important because of two reasons – it's a common use case, and it's also very easy to implement.

There are so many cases where we need to fetch one object only.

And that's interesting – because what happens is that after the fetch request finds the first object, it continues until it finishes to search the rest of the objects.

What we want to do is for the fetch action to stop after it finds the first object, and we can do that easily by setting the `fetchLimit` property:

```
fetchRequest.fetchLimit = 1
```

There are cases where limiting the fetch request can cut the fetch time to half and even more!

Now, I said it's a common use case because many fetch requests try to retrieve a single object. Stopping after the first result can sum up to be a time saver.

String Search Optimization

String-related searches are very popular when working with Core Data. The problem with strings is that they are not only popular but relatively slow to search.

You already saw that predicates containing strings are much more complex than the others, which explains how we can easily fall into nonefficient fetches.

Case-Sensitive Searching

You are already supposed to know by now that Core Data string searches are case sensitive.

You also learned that we could perform case-insensitive searches using the [cd] functions:

```
let predicate = NSPredicate(format: "name ==[cd] %@", "Back in Black")
```

But underneath, things are not that simple.

Let's see a time comparison between case-sensitive and case-insensitive searches:

> *Case Sensitive* – 0.0082

> *Case Insensitive* – 0.0322

Searching with case insensitivity can be almost four times slower! Why does it happen?

If our Core Data debugging is still enabled from before, we can have a look at our console for further information.

For **case-sensitive** searches, we can see the following EXPLAIN statement:

```
EXPLAIN QUERY PLAN SELECT 5, t0.Z_PK, t0.ZNAME FROM ZSONG t0
WHERE  t0.ZNAME = ?
    2 0 0 SEARCH t0 USING COVERING INDEX Z_Song_byName (ZNAME=?)
```

But for case-insensitive searches, we are going to see a different query:

```
EXPLAIN QUERY PLAN SELECT 5, t0.Z_PK, t0.ZNAME FROM ZSONG t0
WHERE NSCoreDataStringCompare( t0.ZNAME , ? , 3, 385, 0)
    2 0 0 SCAN t0 USING COVERING INDEX Z_Song_byName
```

Looking at the preceding code, you can see I marked the relevant change in bold. While the case-insensitive query still uses the index we created, the comparison is made using the NSCoreDataStringCompare, which is much slower.

Now, string comparisons are essential – we use them to find names, IDs, URLs, searches, and more.

So the decision about the type of string search we want to do seems important.

What can we do to handle that?

Well, a known tradeoff is paying with space to get speed. In fact, that's the way indexes work.

To implement that idea in case-insensitive searches, we can add another attribute that holds a lowercase version of the attribute we want to search.

For example, if we have an attribute called "name", we will add another attribute called "namedNormalized".

Since the namedNormalized attribute always holds a lowercase version, we can use that property to perform case-sensitive search:

```
let predicate = NSPredicate(format: "namedNormalized == %@",
"get jude")
```

To keep the normalized text attribute updated, we can override the willSave() NSManagedObject method:

```
public override func willSave() {
    super.willSave()
    self. namedNormalized = name
}
```

Overriding the willSave() method is an elegant solution to ensure our data won't corrupt.

The extra attribute is a great way to eat the cake and leave it whole – we can keep the original text as it is and still perform very quick fetches!

Improve Our Saving

Fetching data is not the only Core Data aspect we can optimize – another action we are doing is saving.

Now, even though saving doesn't look like an action that can be optimized, it is undoubtedly something we can improve.

Batch Saving

I guess that the best saving tip would be "insert many, save once."

You should remember that the saving action is an expensive one. If you have the option to reduce the number of times you push changes to the persistent store, you should lower it to the minimum possible.

Let's look at a simple function that receives an array of contacts and inserts them to the persistent store:

```
func addCOntacts(contacts: [Contact]) throws {
        for contact in contacts {
            let newContact = CoreDataContact(context: context)
            try context.save()
        }
    }
```

We can see the function iterates through the list of contacts, and in each iteration, it inserts a new contact and calls the save() function.

So, for 1000 contacts, the function calls save() 1000 times!

I tried to measure the time my simulator took to save 10000 contacts:

9.1 seconds.

And that's a simulator running on a MacBook Pro M1, yes?

What will happen if we call the save() function once at the end by moving it outside the for each loop?

```
func addCOntacts(contacts: [Contact]) throws {
        for contact in contacts {
            let newContact = CoreDataContact(context: context)
        }
        try context.save() //outside the loop
    }
```

Let's measure the time again:

0.2 seconds!

Inserting 10,000 objects took 0.2 seconds vs. 9 seconds. That's a huge difference!

Remember saving is an expensive operation. Use it with caution, especially with loops.

And that's an action you need to consider where to put – it can be when you go to the background, at the end of a sync operation, or when the user moves out of a screen.

Ordering + Relationships

Do you want to learn more tips that can cut your saving time by half?

Stay tuned.

Let's talk about to-many relationships.

Do you remember we can define a to-many relationship as "ordered"? If you don't have to use that feature and need more power juice, you better give it up and save around 25% time.

Look at these numbers – saving 10,000 objects:

Ordered To-Many Relationship: 0.48 seconds.

Non-ordered To-Many Relationship: 0.36 seconds.

But we can go even further. If we insert these objects, not as part of a relationship, we can earn even more time – 0.25 seconds!

First, we need to understand why it happens. The ordered to-many relationship requires Core Data to maintain linking between the different objects we insert and keep an ordered list, consuming more CPU power.

But the connection Core Data needs to do to maintain the to-many relationship also has its weight, and that's another thing we ditched.

Now, you probably think to yourself, "You said that 'relationships' are one of Core Data's best features," and they are!

But you see, in performance, it's always a tradeoff. On one occasion, we can sacrifice memory, and on another, it will be our comfort as engineers.

In this case, we gave up important Core Data features to speed our savings by 50%. Is it worth it? You decide.

Giving up Core Data features means we need some kind of a replacement. First, we can add an attribute that saves the timestamp of the insertion. That will make it easier for you to sort the objects by their insertion time.

Second, you can maintain a relationship between objects using another attribute representing the connection between the entities.

For example, we can add an attribute named "albumID" for a Song entity, just as we do in SQL tables.

Working with Instruments

All the great tips you got here are not an insurance certificate everything will work flawlessly.

Programs are complex, and managing data is even more complicated.

We can easily get lost in all the tradeoffs and optimizations I showed you.

Lucky us, Apple Instruments is a fantastic tool that can help us get to the bottom of our issues.

A Few Words About Instruments

Instruments is an Xcode tool for memory and performance debugging. Even though it comes as a separate application, Xcode and Instruments work together seamlessly.

Besides memory, CPU, I/O, and network monitoring, Instruments also provides excellent Core Data debugging tools.

Opening Instruments

The best way to start debugging with Instruments is to launch Instruments within Xcode.

One option is to long press the "Run" button in Xcode and choose "Profile." See Figure 9-6.

Figure 9-6. *Running Profile from Xcode*

Another even faster option would be to press ⌘ (Command) + I.

Once we do that, our project will be recompiled, and the Instruments application will be launched.

Instruments opens with a profiling template window, asking you to select the profiling template you want to start with (see Figure 9-7).

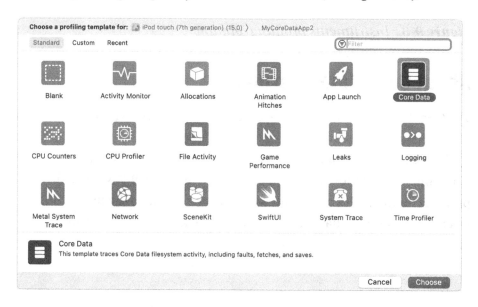

Figure 9-7. *Choose a profiling template in Instruments*

As you can see, there are many profiling templates you can pick from! But this is a Core Data book, so we'll go for the Core Data template. You are more than welcome to explore the other available templates.

After selecting the Core Data template, a new window opens with Core Data instruments available for you to profile (Figure 9-8).

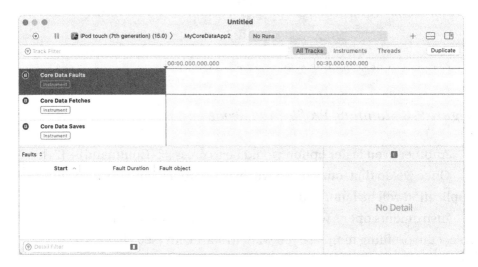

Figure 9-8. *Instruments profiling window*

About Core Data Instruments

The Core Data template has three different instruments we can use – Faults, Fetches, and Saves.

To clear the terminology we use here, each one is called an "instrument," and the "Core Data" you chose in Figure 9-7 is called a profiling template. It's a template because it comes with the three Core Data instruments available today, but you can add more or remove instruments.

Core Data Saves Instrument

The Core Data Saves instrument can help you investigate when your app performs save operations to the persistent store.

Do you remember my example of inserting 10,000 objects into the store? Let's profile that using the Core Data Saves instrument (Figure 9-9).

Figure 9-9. *Core Data Saves instrument profiling*

Our Core Data Saves instrument displays something interesting – it shows that over the first 14 seconds of the app launch, there is a load of save operations done to the persistent store.

To understand precisely what is happening, all we need to do is to select part of the graph and look at the data at the bottom (Figure 9-10).

Figure 9-10. *Investigate save operations in Instruments*

Oh! We can see the list of the save operations, and for each of them, we can also tell **when** it happened, for **how long**, and even **who** called the save operation in our code.

Looking deeply, we see that we call the save() operation for each loop iteration.

Let's do the "fix" we did earlier and move the save operation to the end of the loop. After that, we can rerun Instruments (Figure 9-11).

Figure 9-11. *Running Instruments after the insert objects fix*

Now we see one save operation after half a second. It looks like the problem was fixed!

The number of details we get using the Core Data Saves instrument is just amazing. This instrument can really help you put your thumb on Core Data saving bottlenecks and manage them easily.

Faults and Fetches

Two more Core Data instruments that can be very useful are Fetches and Faults.

As their names suggest, the Core Data Fetches instrument provides information about fetches the app performs, and the Core Data Faults instrument provides information about relationship faulting.

Looking at Figure 9-12, you can see how we can get complete information about Core Data fetching performance, especially when comparing the information to additional related instruments, such as Time Profiler.

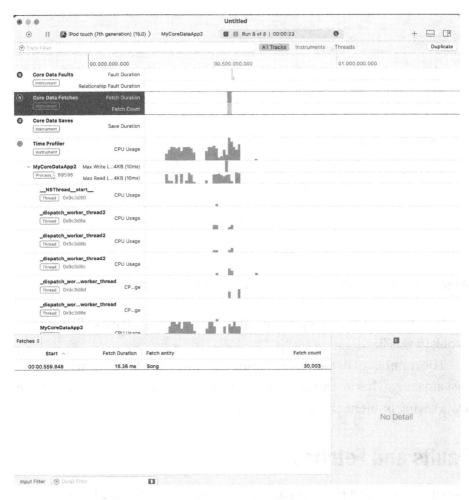

Figure 9-12. *Core Data Fetches and Faults instruments*

Core Data Fetches and Faults instruments can show you high pressure and bottlenecks in your Core Data.

For example, a big faults number may indicate a problematic model scheme or not an optimized fetch request.

And maybe, it's a sign that you need to do batch faulting to be more efficient (just like we learned earlier).

A high number of fetches of the same entity might indicate a narrow predicate you are using or for multiple main contexts trying to fetch data at the same time.

Core Data Instruments can point to an anomaly in the way you work with data and give you a hint of what you can fix.

While it may look a little bit scary at first, Instruments is very friendly.

You should remember that most of the issues you may find there can be easily fixed using the tips you've learned in this chapter.

Summary

I know this chapter is a little bit "weird."

On the one hand, I showed you how Core Data is super-efficient, and on the other hand, I showed you how you could optimize it to your own needs.

But this is how optimizations work.

We want to make the best even better, and it's also a great way to explain how things work underneath, even if you don't need to do anything.

We've learned what faulting is and how to use it to speed our fetches. We also learned how to index our data, speed up our string search, and perform efficient saving operations.

We ended with Instruments – an excellent profiling tool you have in your Xcode.

Now it's time to slow down (again, word game!) and learn how to maintain Core Data for the long run.

CHAPTER 10

Migrations

The computer was born to solve problems that did not exist before.

—Bill Gates

Up until now, we were talking about ways to set up an amazing Core Data infrastructure – how the data model works and how to perform blazingly fast fetch requests.

But nothing stands still. Not us, not our app, and certainly not our data store.

When new app versions come along, we will need to add more features. These features may require data model changes like new entities, attributes, and relationships and even transforming an existing entity to a different one.

But don't worry – Core Data has migration and versioning tools built-in for you to face the most difficult changes!

In this chapter, you will learn

- How migration works

- How to create new versions of your data model

- How to perform a lightweight migration

- How to help Core Data map the changes it needs to do

- How to write a custom migration policy

© Avi Tsadok 2022
A. Tsadok, *Unleash Core Data*, https://doi.org/10.1007/978-1-4842-8211-3_10

Why Does Migration Happen?

To understand why migration and versioning are a "thing" in Core Data, we need to go back to the beginning of the book, when we discussed the "Core Data stack."

Do you remember that? A reminder: The bottom layer of the stack is the **data model**, and on top of it, we have the persistent store.

The persistent store scheme is derived from our data model (this is the importance of the "stack").

In general, Core Data can't open a persistent store if it cannot find a data model that matches the store scheme.

And when that happens, Core Data can't create a stack and throws an exception.

Data Model Changes

When we change the data model while having an existing store, we might bring it to a situation where they don't match.

In this case, we need Core Data to perform migration to the persistent store, so it can be opened using our new data model.

Now let's try to understand precisely what happens under the hood.

Every data model has **a hash identifier** that represents it.

When Core Data creates a persistent store, it attaches the data model hash identifier to that store.

When we perform changes in the data model, a new hash-based identifier is being created, and when we initialize the stack (e.g., on app startup), Core Data **compares the hash attached to the persistent store with the hash of the data model** (Figure 10-1).

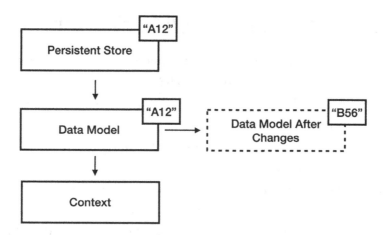

Figure 10-1. *A new hash for the data model after changes*

Looking at Figure 10-1, you can see the data model changes "gave" it a new hash.

In this case, the persistent store needs to go through a **migration process**, as discussed, to adapt its scheme to the new data model.

Now, even though the hash value itself is not interesting, the fact that Core Data decides to migrate the store based on the hash is more interesting.

We can change the data model so that it won't affect the hash value and won't require migration.

For example, **adding a new fetch index** or changing **validation rules** doesn't change the hash value.

If you go to the previous chapter where we discussed the fetch index, you'll see that I told you we need to "trigger" the migration process. We did that by setting a hash modifier because adding a fetch index alone doesn't change the model hash value.

A rule of thumb for you would be a change that affects the persistent store (like adding a new attribute or entity) also modifies the hash value.

Wait! Do You Really Need to Migrate?

Before we go into the hassle of versioning, mapping, and migrations, you need to ask yourself, **Do you really need it**?

Remember Core Data is an object graph framework before it is a persistent framework.

When we discussed the persistent store, we said there are several types of stores we can work with.

One of the stores is "in memory." In this case, Core Data doesn't have a persistent file, and migrations are not required at all.

Having said that, using a persistent store type like SQLite doesn't mean we need to migrate either.

For example, maybe the persistent store goal is mainly for caching purposes.

In the case of caching, we can consider **removing the store and recreating it** upon upgrades.

You should always assume that data migration is always a sensitive and not trivial process, so versioning depends on your use case and app needs.

The Migration Three Steps

Okay, we've changed our data model and must migrate our data store to match the new model version.

Let's go over the steps that happen in every Core Data migration:

- **Compare** the current data model and the new data model we want to migrate to.

- **Infer the changes** and create a mapping model.

- **Perform changes** to the data store according to the mapping model. Also, run a custom migration code if needed.

Notice that the preceding steps are relevant for general data migrations, not only Core Data.

The good news is that Core Data is smart enough to perform most of the migration process in most cases **automatically**.

The bad news? There aren't. I'll start with the most straightforward and automatic way – lightweight migration.

Lightweight Migration

Let's describe our needs again. We have an existing app with a particular data model and a current store with data. We want to make a small but important change to our data model, like **adding a new entity**.

If we simply modify our data model, our app will crash.

We need to migrate from one data model to another data model, and to do that, Core Data needs a new version of our data model.

Adding a New Model Version

Interestingly, when developers start using Core Data in their apps, they discover how deeply Core Data is integrated within Xcode. There are many tools hidden between the different menus.

The same goes with Core Data migration. A built-in process can help you quickly add a new data model version.

To add a new data model, open your data model, go to "Editor," and select "Add Model Version."

Give the new version a name (see Figure 10-2).

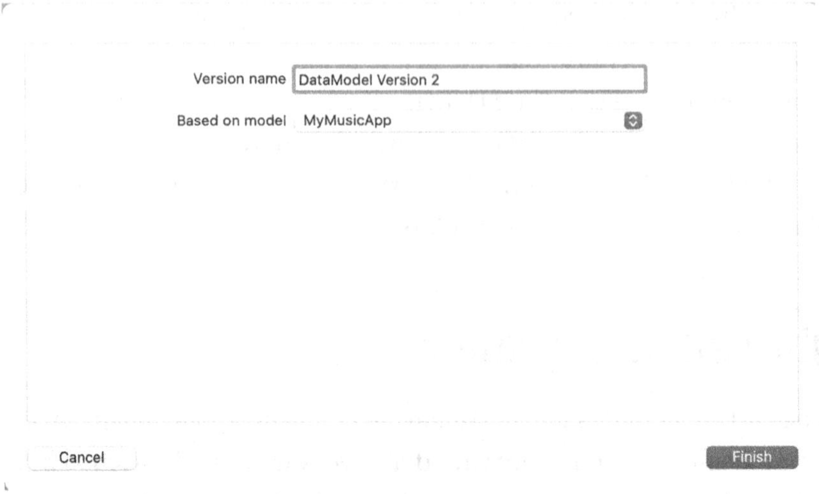
Version name
DataModel Version 2
Based on model
MyMusicApp
Cancel
Finish

Figure 10-2. *Adding a new data model version*

Now go back to your project navigator, and you'll see that your data model is now a package that contains a list of data models (see Figure 10-3).

MyMusicApp
DataModel Version 2
MyMusicApp

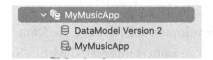

Figure 10-3. *Data model as a package*

Now that we have a new data model version, we can make our changes. At first glance, tapping on the new model version seems like nothing is happening. That's because it's a duplication of the previous version. In the new model, we can add our new entity or attribute.

Modify the New Model Version

Now that we have two data model versions, we can add a new entity as usual.

You should be careful, though – since moving between the different versions is not always clear, be aware of what version you are working on.

For the sake of the example, go and add a new entity called Settings to the latest version.

Our next step will be telling Core Data that the version we've just created is the current and updated version.

Setting the Current Model Version

Look again at Figure 10-3 – do you see there is a green checkmark next to our first version (MyMusicApp)?

This v-mark indicates that MyMusicApp is our current data model version, and that's the version our code supports.

Now we need to set our new version as the "current" one.

To do that, tap on one of the versions and open the file inspector on the right.

You'll see a model version drop-down menu (Figure 10-4).

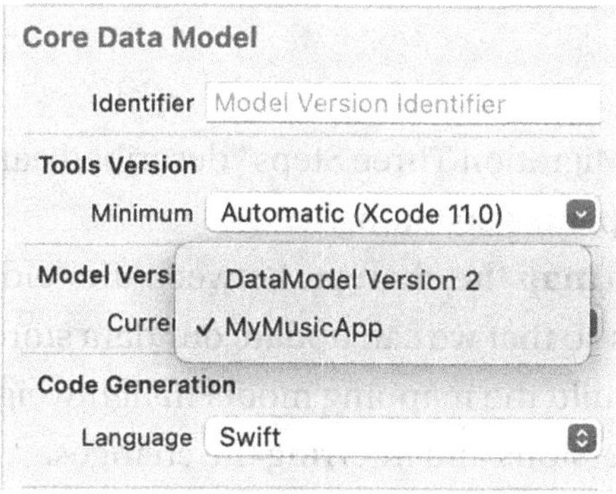

Figure 10-4. *The model version drop-down menu*

Selecting "DataModel Version 2" will move the v-mark to the new version.

Recompile and Open Our App

Now that we have a new model version, we can rebuild our app, open it, and see that our data store now supports the new entity that we have added. Everything in our stack is now synced with each other, and we can safely use the new entity in our code.

About versioning, we can add **as many versions as we want**. Keeping the versions will make sure users with an old version of your app can upgrade to the latest one and will go through the migration process using all the versions you created along the way.

So that's another something you need to keep in mind – an app that has existed for several years may contain a long list of data model versions. It is better to give your versions meaningful and clear names.

For example, a version name can represent the **corresponding change** ("Added Playlist"), the **app version** name ("5.38.2"), or the **creation date** ("APR 22").

When you need to look back and investigate issues, that will pay up.

Mapping

Going back to the "Migration Three Steps" described earlier, we just finished the first step, the versioning.

Now, we want to **map the changes** between the "old" and the "new" data model versions so that we can update our data store.

Core Data can build the mapping model in lightweight migrations by looking at the two versions and inferring the changes.

Let's see how it works.

NSMappingModel

And here's another class you should be familiar with – NSMappingModel. Whenever we perform a migration, Core Data needs an NSMappingModel instance to understand what changes to make to our data store.

Now, look at the following code snippet:

```
let oldModelURL = Bundle.main.url(forResource: "MyDataModel.
momd/ModelVersion1", withExtension: "mom")!
let oldModel = NSManagedObjectModel(contentsOf: oldModelURL)!
let newModelURL = Bundle.main.url(forResource: "MyDataModel.
momd/ModelVersion2", withExtension: "mom")!
let newModel = NSManagedObjectModel(contentsOf: newModelURL)!
let model = try NSMappingModel.inferredMappingModel(forSourceMo
del: oldModel, destinationModel: newModel)
```

Here are a few things we can learn from here:

- Look how I created a URL for a model version – that's the way of doing that. Remember that the data model is a package once we have multiple versions. Also, look at the extension – mom. mom is the compiled version of xcdatamodel.

- Once we have a URL, we can initialize an NSManagedObjectModel instance. I know we haven't talked much about this class, but now we have a perfect example of how to use it.

- The inferredMappingModel method returns an NSMappingModel instance by looking at the two versions. If the function throws an error, we understand that Core Data has failed to infer a mapping model.

Now that we have a mapping instance, we can examine it.

Let's look at the property entitiyMappingsByName (Figure 10-5).

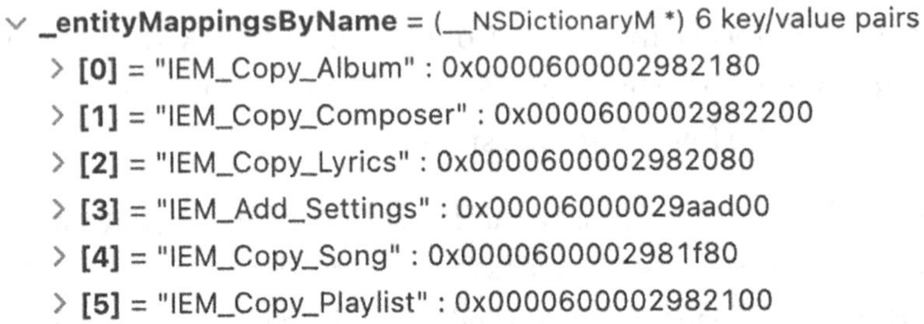

> ⌄ **_entityMappingsByName** = (__NSDictionaryM *) 6 key/value pairs
> > [0] = "IEM_Copy_Album" : 0x0000600002982180
> > [1] = "IEM_Copy_Composer" : 0x0000600002982200
> > [2] = "IEM_Copy_Lyrics" : 0x0000600002982080
> > [3] = "IEM_Add_Settings" : 0x00006000029aad00
> > [4] = "IEM_Copy_Song" : 0x0000600002981f80
> > [5] = "IEM_Copy_Playlist" : 0x0000600002982100

Figure 10-5. *EntitiyMappingsByName property*

We can tell that the mapping model assumes we need to copy the Album, Composer, Lyrics, Song, and Playlist entities.

We also see that the mapping model inferred that we need to add a new entity named Settings. This is precisely what we did in our data model.

Core Data recognized it as a new entity.

Well done, Core Data!

Enable Lightweight Migration

I want to clarify something before we continue – the previous step of instancing a mapping model is not required.

I showed that step for two reasons: First is to demonstrate how Core Data can infer simple changes between versions. Second, you'll be able to check if Core Data can do that.

If Core Data fails to infer a mapping model, it means that our changes were "too radical" for it to analyze.

We will learn soon how to handle these situations.

The next step of performing the migration is also done automatically in lightweight migration.

To ensure everything is done automatically, we need to verify that two essential properties are set to true.

Let's go back to the NSPersistentContainer. (Remember that? If not, go back to the beginning of the book.)

The NSPersistentContainer has a property named persistentStoreDescriptions.

You already see a returning pattern here – many of the Core Data configurations are called "Description", which can help you remember.

To enable both automatic migration and automatic mapping, we need to do the following:

```
let description = NSPersistentStoreDescription(url:(cont
description.shouldMigrateStoreAutomatically = true
description.shouldInferMappingModelAutomatically = true
container.persistentStoreDescriptions =  [description]
```

Look at the two properties I marked in bold. You can easily understand by their names what they should do.

One thing is critical here – this should be done **before the container loads the persistent store**, so it is better to do that right after creating a container.

Lightweight Migration Use Cases

Lightweight migration is not magic – at the end, Core Data performs a simple diff logic and produces a mapping model.

So, to understand when Core Data can perform a lightweight migration, we can turn on our logic and think when it is possible to infer the changes.

Core Data can perform lightweight migration in the following changes:

- Adding or removing attributes/entities

- Changing an attribute from optional to non-optional and vice versa

- Adding or changing relationships

These look like trivial changes!

What About Renaming?

Core Data lightweight migration supports entity and attribute renaming, but that is a little bit trickier.

Let's try to rename the entity Song to Track and see how Core Data infers a mapping model (Figure 10-6).

```
∨ _entityMappingsByName = (__NSDictionaryM *) 7 key/value pairs
  > [0] = "IEM_Transform_Album" : 0x000060000165d980
  > [1] = "IEM_Add_Track" : 0x000060000165d680
  > [2] = "IEM_Transform_Composer" : 0x000060000165da00
  > [3] = "IEM_Transform_Lyrics" : 0x000060000165d800
  > [4] = "IEM_Remove_Song" : 0x000060000165da80
  > [5] = "IEM_Transform_Playlist" : 0x000060000165d780
  > [6] = "IEM_Add_Settings" : 0x000060000165d600
```

Figure 10-6. *Renaming Song to Track*

Core Data succeeded in inferring a mapping model, but it's not the mapping model that we want.

The migration tool "saw" that there is a Song entity in the old model, but now it is gone. Instead, there is a new entity called Track.

So naturally, the mapping model removes the Song entity and adds a new entity – Track.

Some of the other entities are required to update their relationships because of the change, and therefore we see the Transform actions.

So what do we do?

We need to tell Core Data that Track and Song are actually the same entity. To do that, we need to link between them, and that can be done using something called a "renaming ID."

Let's go back to our data model editor and open our old data model version.

Now, tap on the Song entity and look at the inspector pane on the right (Figure 10-7).

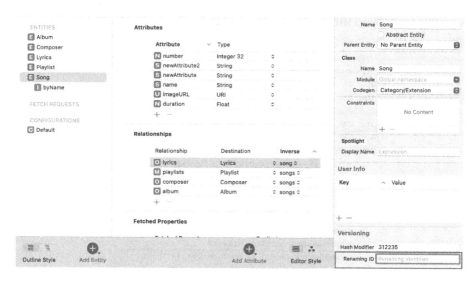

Figure 10-7. *Renaming ID in the data model editor*

Where does it come from, ha?

Do you see? In this book, we explore new things every two to three pages so that you won't get bored.

The "Renaming ID" text field, which is part of the Versioning section, aims to solve the issue we just discussed – how to give an entity/attribute/ relationship **identity in case of renaming**.

You can give any renaming ID that you want, as long as

–   The renaming ID is **unique** (you can't provide the same ID for two entities).

–   The entity in the old and the new model version contains the **same renaming ID**. Filling the renaming ID in one of the versions only doesn't help Core Data with the mapping process.

In this case, I gave the Song/Track entity name change a renaming ID of "1".

241

Now, let's try to infer a mapping model and see what happens (Figure 10-8).

```
∨ _entityMappingsByName = (__NSDictionaryM *) 6 key/value pairs
  > [0] = "IEM_Transform_Playlist" : 0x0000600002c6ec00
  > [1] = "IEM_Transform_Album" : 0x0000600002c6ee00
  > [2] = "IEM_Transform_Composer" : 0x0000600002c6ee80
  > [3] = "IEM_Add_Settings" : 0x0000600002c6ea80
  ∨ [4] = "IEM_Transform_1" : 0x0000600002c6eb00
      > key = (__NSCFString *) "IEM_Transform_1"
      ∨ value = (NSEntityMapping?) 0x0000600002c6eb00
          > baseNSObject@0 (NSObject)
          > _reserved = (void *) NULL
          > _reserved1 = (void *) NULL
          > _mappingsByName = (id) 0x0
          > _name = (__NSCFString *) "IEM_Transform_1"
            _mappingType = (unsigned long long) 5
          > _sourceEntityName = (NSTaggedPointerString *) "Song"
          > _sourceEntityVersionHash = (_NSInlineData *) 32 bytes
          > _destinationEntityName = (NSTaggedPointerString *) "Track"
          > _destinationEntityVersionHash = (_NSInlineData *) 32 bytes
          > _sourceExpression = (NSFetchRequestExpression?) 0x0000600002144...
          > _userInfo = (__NSFrozenDictionaryM *) 0x60000023a100
          > _entityMigrationPolicyClassName = (id) 0x0
          > _attributeMappings = (__NSFrozenArrayM *) 0x600000c1da70
```

Figure 10-8. *Mapping model for renaming an entity*

Now that's a totally different mapping model.

Instead of removing Song and adding Track, the mapping model now has a new mapping called "Tranform_1", where "1" is the renaming ID we provided for both entities.

We can also see the source entity name ("Song") and the destination entity name ("Track"), and that is another confirmation that the mapping model works as expected.

So renaming an entity (or a relationship) is possible in Core Data migration. It just requires us to apply common sense and link the entities together.

Custom Mapping Migration

Okay, so we already realize that Core Data is outstanding. It can infer a mapping model easily when noticeable changes happen.

But what should we do when our changes **are not that obvious**?

For example, what happens when we want to change an attribute type or transfer an attribute into a new object with a relationship?

We need to **help** Core Data create the mapping model for the migration in this case.

It may be a small assistant for Core Data to understand what to do in most cases.

Custom mapping migration is done using a custom mapping model we can create that gives us complete control of the mapping itself.

First Step: Create a New Version and Lock It

The first step is doing what we've learned in lightweight migration, and that's creating a new data model version.

Trivial, right? Right. But I mention it because it has a small catch.

We cannot modify the data model once we create a custom mapping model. The mapping model is "locked" to the data model version when created, so the first step you need to do is to make sure you have a new, finalized data model version to migrate to.

Let's assume we have a Song entity with a Note attribute for demonstration purposes.

What we want the migration process to do is to create a new entity named Note that has a one-to-one relationship with Song.

Of course, the challenge is how to transfer the Note attribute values from Song objects to the new Note entity.

Figure 10-9 demonstrates the change we want to do.

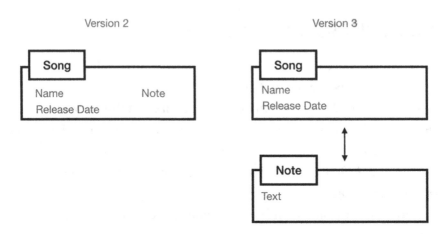

Figure 10-9. *Breaking Note to its own entity*

The new data model version should contain the Note entity with a String attribute called Text.

At this point, don't forget to set the newly created version as the "current version," just like we've learned in lightweight migration.

Our next step will be to map the "old" Song->Note value to the "new" Note->Text value.

Core Data can't infer that from our version; therefore, we need to create a custom mapping model.

Create a Custom Mapping Model

If you remember from the lightweight migration process, Core Data needs a mapping model to perform a migration between versions.

Using Xcode, we have the option to write our own mapping model.

To add a new mapping model file, choose File ➤ New and select the Mapping Model template (Figure 10-10):

Choose a template for your new file:

iOS   macOS   watchOS   tvOS   ⊖ mapping   ⊗

Core Data

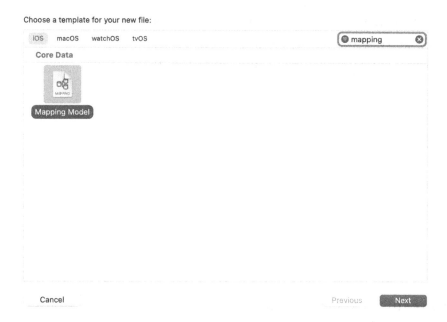

Mapping Model

Cancel   Previous   Next

Figure 10-10. *Adding a new Mapping Model template*

Since a mapping model maps "source" and "destination" data versions, the next step would be to select them as part of the mapping model setup (Figure 10-11).

Mapping Model Source Data Model   Mapping Model Target Data Model

Please choose the Source Data Model for this Mapping Model   Please choose the Target Data Model for this Mapping Model

MyCoreDataApp2   MyCoreDataApp2
  MyCoreDataApp2   MyCoreDataApp2
    MyDataModel.xcdatamodeld   MyDataModel.xcdatamodeld
      MyCoreDataApp4.xcdatamodel   MyCoreDataApp4.xcdatamodel
      MyCoreDataApp3.xcdatamodel   MyCoreDataApp3.xcdatamodel
      MyCoreDataApp2.xcdatamodel   MyCoreDataApp2.xcdatamodel

Cancel   Previous   Next   Cancel   Previous   Next

Figure 10-11. *Select "source" and "destination" data model versions*

245

Now we need to name the new mapping model. It is best to give it a meaningful name like "MappingFrom3To4".

Let's open the new mapping model (Figure 10-12).

Figure 10-12. *Mapping model*

Looks like a familiar UI, ha? Well, the mapping model editor looks like the data model editor. But it's not coincidental – after all, we are dealing with entities, attributes, and relationships, so we can expect similar screens.

If you remember how we examine the NSMappingModel, you may find some terms familiar – SongToSong, LyricsToLyrics, and more.

These are the patterns that are being used in a mapping model when dealing with converting one entity to another.

Tapping on one of the entity mappings reveals how the mapping is handled – using value expressions (Figure 10-13).

Figure 10-13. *Album entity mapping*

As you probably see from Figure 10-13, all the attribute mapping stays the same for now – the title attribute value will be the old value (`$source.title`), and that's true for the rest.

The relationship mapping is even more interesting, but it also stays the same. It takes the value of the song from the SongToSong mapping and saves it into songs – that is basically what is happening.

Now that we understand what mapping is and the basic terms, we can move on to our mission – take over the world. And we'll start that mission by mapping the note value in Song to the new entity Note.

Map Song->Note to NoteObject

Okay, we reached the money time! We need to perform four steps to map the Song's Note to a NoteObject.

Let's start with the first and the simplest one – set the source of the mapping.

Set the Source to Song

Looking back at Figure 10-12, we have a new mapping named "Note". That's because Core Data identified that the new data model version has a new entity called Note, and therefore it created a new, corresponding mapping (which is currently empty).

Tapping on the new mapping reveals an entity mapping on the right pane (Figure 10-14).

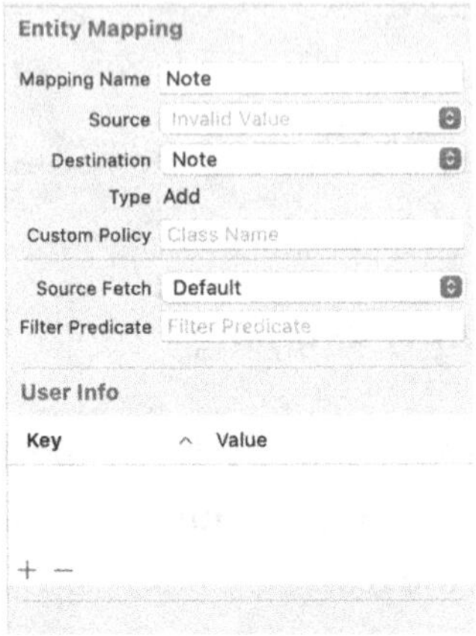

Figure 10-14. *New entity mapping*

Looking at the mapping information, we see that we have a "destination," which is the current entity, but no information about the source.

Our goal is to map data from the Song entity, **so we set the Source field to Song**.

Doing that changes the mapping name to SongToNote automatically. How clever is that, ha?

That was a simple step.

Let's continue with modifying the attribute value.

Set Attribute Mapping

Our next step is also a simple one. Look again at Figure 10-12 – we have a new attribute called "content" that is supposed to contain the note data.

We need to map the original note value to the content attribute.

To do that, we'll fill the Value Expression field with the following:

```
$source.note
```

No need to explain that, right? I promised you that was an easy step as well.

But we still need to understand what is happening here.

This step not only copies the note attribute value into the content attribute but also creates a new NoteObject object for every Song object.

We still have one step missing. Can you guess what it is?

I'll tell you – we need to map the relationship between our Song and the new NoteObject.

That's our next step, which is a little bit trickier.

Relationship Mapping

Remember that copying the note value from one entity to another is only half the job.

It doesn't mean anything about the relationship between the Song entity and the new NoteObject entity. Core Data is intelligent, but it's not a mind reader.

Under the attribute mapping, we can see we have another mapping category – relationship mapping.

And we already have a relationship mapping here called song (see Figure 10-15).

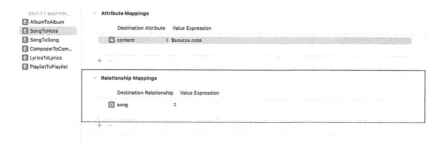

Figure 10-15. *Relationship mapping*

What we will do here is to map the "source" of the SongToNote mapping (which is the Song entity) to the relationship called a song.

Confused? I told you this step is a little bit tricky.

Let's move forward, and it will be more apparent.

Tap on "song" under Relationship Mappings and look on the right pane (Figure 10-16).

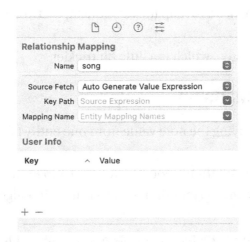

Figure 10-16. *Relationship mapping pane*

Unlike entity mapping, which copies values, we need to connect objects in relationship mapping.

In that case, we actually need to write a function that fetches relevant objects to connect.

Don't worry – the relationship mapping pane can help you with auto-generating an expression based on your input.

In the "Key Path" field, write "$source", and in Mapping Name, choose "SongToSong" mapping. Make sure it's like what we see in Figure 10-17.

Figure 10-17. *Relationship mapping pane filled*

And now for the best part in this chapter, look back on the relationship mapping, and you can see that Xcode filled the Value Expression field for you with the following:

```
FUNCTION($manager, "destinationInstancesForEntityMappingNamed:
sourceInstances:" , "SongToSong", $source)
```

Sure, we are happy Xcode writes code and expressions for us, but what does it mean?

$manager – Every migration has a migration instance of class NSMigrationManager that handles the migration process. $manager is a reference to that manager.

The destinationInstancesForEntityMappingNamed:sourceInsta nces: is one of the NSMigrationManager functions. It returns instances created in the destination in a specific mapping.

The following two parameters are, in fact, this function parameter. We first pass the relevant mapping (SongToSong) and its source (Song).

To summarize that part in English, Core Data will go to the mapping SongToSong, take its source (Song), return all its instances, and link them to the NoteObject using that relationship.

251

Suggestion   Open a new project and try this yourself. In most cases, you'll see that it is simpler than it looks when reading that in a book.

Disable Automatically Inferring a Mapping Model

We spent a few pages mapping the changes ourselves because we knew that Core Data could not do that alone.

What we need to do now is to tell Core Data that we handled it ourselves and it doesn't need to infer a mapping model automatically.

When we discussed lightweight migration, I told you that we need to make sure that inferring a mapping model is automatically enabled.

Now, we need to do the opposite – to disable it using the same code:

```
let description = NSPersistentStoreDescription(url:(cont
description.shouldMigrateStoreAutomatically = true
description.shouldInferMappingModelAutomatically = false
container.persistentStoreDescriptions = [description]
```

Notice we are still leaving the automatic migration enabled since it's precisely what we want – for Core Data to migrate automatically, but the mapping should be our responsibility.

Custom Migration Policy

The mapping model is a remarkable piece of tool – we can easily create custom mapping migrations using a friendly interface. When looking at other IDEs, most of them don't offer that experience.

But there are times that even a mapping model editor is not enough and we want to take complete control of how our migrations are handled.

Lucky us, Core Data provides an additional layer of control, and we can define a specific migration policy for a specific mapping.

Splitting the Song Entity

At this point, you should know two things about me:

- I always explain things using examples.

- The examples are (almost) always around our fantastic music app.

And this case is no different. Our wish now is to create two different entities – LongSong and ShortSong.

And what we want to do is to take all of our Song objects and **split them** into our new entities.

A song with a duration longer than 3 seconds will be transferred to a LongSong, and a shorter song will be transferred to a ShortSong.

That may not be the most logical step in a music app, but that's only for the sake of the example.

New Model Version and Mapping Model

The good news about what we need to do is that the first steps are practically the same as previous migration techniques:

- Creating a new data model version

- Adding two more entities – LongSong and ShortSong (with relevant attributes, of course)

- Creating a mapping model

What we want to do now is to "ride" on the SongToSong migration process and to do all our magic there.

You might wonder why I chose to use the SongToSong mapping when we don't map Song to Song, eh?

If that's the case, perhaps now is the time to understand what SongToSong actually means.

The SongToSong mapping means that the Core Data migration manager goes for each Song instance and expects to receive a Song instance or another one.

If we use a SongToLongSong mapping file, Core Data will create a LongSong instance for every Song we have, which is not what we want.

Create Our Migration Policy

So how do we define a custom migration code for SongToSong?

Let's go back to the mapping model we created and tap on the SongToSong entity mapping.

Now, look at the inspector pane (Figure 10-18).

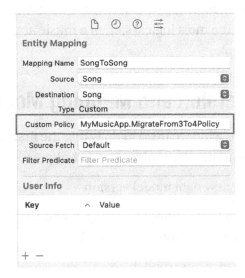

Figure 10-18. *SongToSong mapping inspector*

Oh, what do we have here? A custom policy!

The custom policy is built upon a module and a class.

In this case, the module is MyMusicApp, and the class is MigrateFrom3To4Policy.

When Core Data needs to perform a SongToSong migration, it creates an instance of MigrateFrom3To4Policy to know how to handle the process.

MigrateFrom3To4Policy is a subclass of NSEntityMigrationPolicy and has all the information required to perform the migration.

Let's dive into the coding part.

NSEntityMigrationPolicy

In the end, we need to remember that we are all engineers. Before everything else, our language is Swift and butter.

Writing a custom migration process should be intuitive for you, even more than UI.

Let's add a new Swift file with the following:

```
class MigrateFrom3To4Policy: NSEntityMigrationPolicy {

    override func createDestinationInstances(forSource
    sInstance: NSManagedObject, in mapping: NSEntityMapping,
    manager: NSMigrationManager) throws {
            }

}
```

If we go back to Figure 10-18, we can see that MigrateFrom3To4Policy is the same name we wrote under the Custom Policy field.

When Core Data uses the provided mapping model, it will instantiate the MigrateFrom3To4Policy class to perform the SongToSong mapping process.

One of the methods our class overrides is createDestinationInstances, which is responsible for creating instances according to incoming objects from the migrator.

Let's see its parameters and what we can do with them:

- sInstance - The source instance we want to **migrate from**. In the case of SongToSong it will be a Song instance.

- mapping - The relevant **mapping model**.

- manager - The migration manager that manages the migration process.

Before we fill that method with our migration code, we need to understand how the migration process works at this point.

At first, Core Data creates a new persistent store that replaces the old persistent store your app already uses.

The new data model version we created earlier is currently being used only for mapping the changes. At this point in time, we **don't have access to the new version**, and this is something we need to keep in mind.

As a result, classes such as LongSong are not available for us even though it doesn't mean we can't handle it, using NSEntityDescription.

Moreover, the new persistent store has a context of its own. If we want to insert new objects, we should **use that context** with the help of the migration manager.

Once the migration process finishes successfully, Core Data **replaces** the old persistent store with the new one it created.

Now, it's time to see it in code:

```
override func createDestinationInstances(forSource sInstance:
NSManagedObject, in mapping: NSEntityMapping, manager:
NSMigrationManager) throws {

        let destinationContext = manager.destinationContext
        let duration = sInstance.value(forKey: "duration") as?
        Float ?? 0.0
```

```
    let name = sInstance.value(forKey: "name") as?
    String ?? ""
    let id = sInstance.value(forKey: "id") as? UUID

    var newSong: NSManagedObject?

    if duration > 3.0 {
        newSong = NSEntityDescription.
        insertNewObject(forEntityName: "LongSong", into:
        destinationContext)
    } else {
        newSong = NSEntityDescription.
        insertNewObject(forEntityName: "ShortSong", into:
        destinationContext)
    }

    newSong?.setValue(id, forKey: "id")
    newSong?.setValue(name, forKey: "name")
}
```

The code is short but elegant and simple.

We use entity description and setValue/getValue to work in an environment free of NSManagedObject subclasses.

You already should be familiar with this approach – we've learned it in one of the book's early chapters.

But why do we need to go back and use setValue/getValue?

Core Data indeed has two persistent stores, but the Objective-C runtime **hasn't loaded the new model** version yet because Core Data hasn't finished migration.

Another important thing to be aware of is that we don't call the super method in the preceding example.

Our new context provided by the manager comes completely empty.

The default behavior of `createDestinationInstances` is to **create an instance of the target entity** (in this example Song) and insert it into the new context.

We don't create a Song instance at all in our example – we only create `LongSong` and `ShortSong`.

This means that the new context won't have any Song entities.

In this case, converting all songs to `LongSong` and `ShortSong` is probably the desired behavior, but it may not be the case for other processes, so this is something you should be aware of.

Removing the Song Entity from the Model Version

Looking back to our migration code, we understand now that we don't have any Song entities once the migration processes end.

Does this mean we can safely remove the Song entity from our new data model version?

In one word, **yes**! In more than one word, yes, but you need to fix your code accordingly.

What I did in this book is to tell you how wonderful it is to use `NSManagedObject` subclasses in your codebase and how convivence it is to use `"song.title"` or `"song.album"` in your project.

But the minute your new, non-Song data model version is the "current" version, the Xcode compiler doesn't recognize Song as a class.

So, yes, you can remove old entities, but you should also adapt your codebase to the new data model version. And you know what? That's okay. A migration process is not only the migration of our data but also a migration of our code that needs to start using the new model version.

Summary

In general, data migrations are considered complex and sensitive tasks.

Lucky us, Apple made Core Data migrations simple, especially when we only need minor changes to our scheme.

In this chapter, you've learned about model versions, lightweight migrations, custom mapping, and migration policies.

In the next chapter, we will talk about how Core Data can be integrated with other modules and services.

CHAPTER 11

Building a Custom Store Type

Code never lies, comments sometimes do.

—Ron Jeffries

This chapter is a little bit different than the others. While all the other chapters dealt with practical examples and approaches, this chapter is more theoretical.

Even though this chapter contains many code examples, its primary goal is to reveal how **Core Data stores work underneath**.

In this chapter, you will learn

- What it means "creating a custom store"

- What are the possible use cases of creating your own store

- Differences between atomic and incremental stores

- How to register a new custom store

- Building an atomic store

- Building an incremental store

© Avi Tsadok 2022
A. Tsadok, *Unleash Core Data*, https://doi.org/10.1007/978-1-4842-8211-3_11

Custom Store: What Exactly Does It Mean?

Okay, so a quick reminder of what a Core Data stack looks like.

We have three main components – the **data model**, a **data store**, and the **context**.

Look at Figure 11-1 to remember.

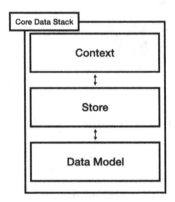

Figure 11-1. *A reminder of the Core Data stack*

Drilling down to the "Store" component, we know that we have four types of such a store – three **atomic** (XML, binary, and in-memory) and one **incremental** (SQLite).

Now, it's time to reveal that we have the option to **create a custom store** by subclassing either NSIncrementalStore or NSAtomicStore.

These two classes let you write your own store type and basically control how Core Data saves, fetches, and optimizes local data.

For example, you can write a store that can **work with CSV** files instead of SQLite or even a store that **syncs independently with a web service**. In fact, almost anything is possible once you have control.

Why Do We Need That?

In most cases, you don't. The four store types that come with Core Data are suitable for most of your needs.

But there are a couple of reasons you need to know how to create your own data store.

One thing to understand is that using your own custom data store doesn't mean additional modifications for the rest of your stack. The data model and the context don't know they are working with a custom data store, and the rest of your codebase stays the same.

It means that your store is easily replaceable, so there is no need to worry!

Rely on Your Technology

SQLite is a very efficient way of storing data, and it is no coincidence that it was chosen as the go-to DB in many mobile applications.

But it doesn't mean that it's the only way of managing data on a mobile device.

For example, there are great solutions for implementing a NoSQL datastore on iOS, and writing a custom store is a way of **connecting your Core Data to a different type of store**.

Cross-Platform Support

If you work with Android developers in the same team, there are cases where there is a requirement for both platforms to work on the same data file format.

In many situations, aligning all platforms to work on the same formats and technology is essential to team success.

Lucky us, by using a custom store type, we can work on the same format and still use the excellent Core Data features.

Migrating from an Old Persistent Store

If you are working on an existing app that doesn't have Core Data implemented yet, but the app already has a data store, creating a custom store may be a good starting point.

Migrating from an old persistent layer can always be cumbersome, so this method can ease the migration pain.

Connect the Persistent Store Directly to a Web Service

Because we have complete control of how the store behaves, an excellent idea would be to **bind it directly to your backend service**.

That may seem like a weird idea, especially when you think of the "separation of concerns" principle.

But there are ways you can connect your store directly to a web service without making it too coupled, like dependency injection.

This is an exciting approach we can explore later.

To Explore Another Stack Component

Learning how to create a custom store can reveal some Core Data secrets of how it works underneath.

It basically means that you take responsibility for fetching, saving, and faulting.

It's a process that gives another overview of Core Data from a different angle and can only make you a better iOS developer.

Perhaps, that's the best reason to try and learn it.

NSIncrementalStore vs. NSAtomicStore

As mentioned, Core Data stores are divided into two types – **atomic** and **incremental**.

How to choose which type of store to create?

It depends on your needs – each store type has its drawbacks and advantages.

Atomic stores favor simplicity over performance. In atomic stores, we load all the data to memory, and each time we need to perform changes (insert/update/delete), we have to save all the data.

Therefore, it's a straightforward store to manage, but it also consumes maximum memory.

Atomic stores are relevant when we need to base our data on JSON, XML, or CSV files.

Also, notice that these files cannot be too big – in that case, consider using the incremental store.

Compared to atomic stores, incremental stores are more complicated to implement. They require us to handle all the faulting and optimizations ourselves and are meant for those who **favor performance over simplicity**.

Incremental stores are used where we have big data files or other special async data fetching, such as HTTP requests.

Both store types allow us to create basically anything we want as a persistent store. We just need to understand how they work.

How Do They Work?

Before we move on, I want to explain the basic way stores work in Core Data, and it's even simpler than you think.

First, let's talk about Core Data's responsibility and what is yours.

Core Data is in charge of

- — Initializing our store

- — Handling the fetching, including predicates

- — Managing the different contexts for us

You, on the other hand, need to

- — Create objects based on your data.

- — Generate object IDs.

- — Define the store metadata information.

- — Provide additional data information when requested.

In other words, what we need to do as developers is handle the connection between the Core Data framework and our backing store, whatever it might be.

Before we start setting up an atomic store, let's look at its superclass – NSPersistentStore.

NSPersistentStore

NSPersistentStore is the base class for all Core Data persistent stores. NSPersistentStore is also the superclass of NSIncrementalStore and NSAtomicStore, and if we want to create our own store, we need to subclass one of these classes.

To create a new atomic store, we will create a new subclass called MyAtomicStore:

```
class MyAtomicStore: NSAtomicStore
```

As I said earlier, we don't initialize the stores ourselves – that's the Core Data framework's job.

Our job is to register them and tell Core Data what type of store we want them to load.

Every store has metadata that contains both a type and UUID.

The metadata information helps Core Data initialize the new store, manage its migration, share it between extensions, and, in general, take care of our store overtime.

Let's add the following to our MyAtomicStore class:

```
static let type = "MyAtomicStore" //1
static let uuid = "My Atomic Store for songs" //2
static let storeType = NSPersistentStore.StoreType
(rawValue: type) //3

static let storeDescription : NSPersistentStoreDescription = {
     let desc = NSPersistentStoreDescription()
      desc.type = type
      return desc
  }() //4

  override var type: String {
      return MyAtomicStore.type
  }

  override var metadata: [String : Any]! {
      get {
          return [NSStoreTypeKey : MyAtomicStore.type,
          NSStoreUUIDKey: MyAtomicStore.uuid]
      }
      set {
          super.metadata = newValue
      }
  }
}
```

We started with declaring a type and a UUID based on these values, and we also created a storeType and a store description. Both will be used when we set up our Core Data container.

Notice that the overridden methods and variables are mandatory for creating a custom store. Don't worry – we have plenty of methods to override for the store to work, and that's a good start.

Now that we have our metadata, we can register our store to Core Data.

Registering the New Store

To ensure Core Data loads our store, we need to perform two steps: register and then load it.

To register the store we created, we will add the following line to applicationDidFinishLaunchingWithOptions:

```
NSPersistentStoreCoordinator.registerStoreClass(MyAtomicStore.
self, type: MyAtomicStore.storeType)
```

Our next step is to add the store description we created earlier to the Core Data container **before we load it**:

```
let container = NSPersistentContainer(name: "MySongsApp")
container.persistentStoreDescriptions = [MyAtomicStore.
storeDescription]
                container.loadPersistentStores(completion
                Handler: { (storeDescription, error) in
```

If everything goes well, our container will be loaded without any issues.

NSAtomicStore

Now that our store is loaded, let's dive into the store itself.

Atomic stores are different from incremental stores because they hold all the data in memory.

That makes them simple and fast, but not that efficient in terms of memory, especially when dealing with big stores.

It's no surprise that the primary task will be loading all the data to memory.

Mapping the Data

So the first thing we want to do is to create a dictionary that maps all the instances to a unique value such as UUID:

```
var objectMapping = [UUID : NSManagedObjectID]()
```

Notice we are not mapping the objects themselves but instead their object IDs. Do you remember why?

The reason is that a managed object is not something that the store holds or creates – this is part of the managed object context's job.

That's why it's so enriched to learn how to create a data store of your own – you finally get to know how things are working behind the scenes, and we are only getting started.

Loading All the Data

As I said earlier (and probably even a few times), atomic stores hold all their data from the start.

So one of the methods that are getting called when the store is loaded is load():

```
override func load() throws {
```

The load() method is part of the NSAtomicStore class, and you **must override** it when creating your own atomic store.

If our store works with some sort of a CSV file, that's the time for us to go to the file and load all its records.

Let's look at the steps we need to do to make everything connected:

–   Load the CSV (or any other persistent file or data) file into the memory.

–   Loop all its rows.

–   For every row

    •   Generate a new referenceID.

    •   Generate a new objectID based on the referenceID.

    •   Create a new cache node (that's our "object").

    •   Fill the cache node with data.

    •   Map the objectID to its referenceID.

    •   Add the cache node to the store.

It looks like a lot of work, ha? Well, it's not that much considering this is most of the job you are going to do when creating your own store.

Here is a basic, functional load() method:

```
override func load() throws {

        let songs = rowsFromCSV()
        var set = Set<NSAtomicStoreCacheNode>()

        for songDict in songs {
            guard let songDesc = self.
            persistentStoreCoordinator?.managedObjectModel.
            entitiesByName["Song"] else{ return }

            let uuid = UUID()
            let name = songDict["name"] as! String
            let objectID = self.objectID(for: songDesc,
            withReferenceObject: uuid)
```

```
        let cacheNode = NSAtomicStoreCacheNode(objectID:
        objectID)
        cacheNode.setValue(name, forKey: "name")
        songsMapping[uuid] = objectID
        set.insert(cacheNode)
    }

    addCacheNodes(set)
}
```

Please go line by line and try to understand what is happening according to the step I listed before.

More Insights

Don't worry. I won't leave you in the dark with the code I just showed you.

Here are a couple of things you should know.

For every row in the CSV, our goal is to create something called **a cache node**. A cache node represents a **record** in our store, which is where we hold our data once we load it from the local file.

When we insert a new record to our store, we are basically inserting a new cache node.

To create a cache node, we need to provide an objectID. Up until now, we only read objectID values but never generated one.

Now, we will generate an objectID using an NSAtomicStore built-in method:

```
let objectID = self.objectID(for: songDesc,
withReferenceObject: uuid)
```

After creating the cache node, we can set its values using a regular setValue() function:

```
cacheNode.setValue(name, forKey: "name")
```

This is the place where we fill our store with information from the CSV. A good tip would be to get the names of the key attributes out from the entity description instead of making them hard-coded.

It may look like an over-engineering task, but it pays off in the long run.

What About Relationships?

Core Data isn't just a persistent store but also an object graph. It means that our new store needs to **manage relationships between different objects**.

Remember that our "objects" are actually the cache nodes we just created. To implement a relationship, all we need to do is to connect one cache node to another:

```
let albumCacheNode = NSAtomicStoreCacheNode(objectID:
albumObjectID)
// filling the Albume node with data
songNode.setValue(albumCacheNode, forKey: "album")
```

Don't forget that the album node is just a standard cache node – we need to generate an objectID (based on the entity description), map it, and insert it to the store, exactly as we did with the song node.

Adding a New Object

Our store probably needs to support adding new objects.

After we know how to load all the data from our CSV file and convert it to nodes, adding new information should be quite easy, but it requires us to perform additional work.

When Core Data inserts and manipulates objects, our store doesn't do anything – remember, the context is the application sandbox. Our store enters the picture only when the context save() method is called.

In this case, we need to do three things: **generate** a new reference ID, **create** a new cache node, and **save** the data to the CSV file.

Generate a New Reference ID

It looks like we have already been there, no?

I told you things will be more and more familiar from now on.

When the Core Data context (now it is your client) asks to insert a new object, the first thing we need to do is to **return a reference object**.

The reference object must be unique, and it should be derived from the object values.

If not, we need to keep mapping it.

To return a new reference object, implement the newReferenceObject method:

```
override func newReferenceObject(for managedObject:
NSManagedObject) -> Any {
    let uuid = UUID()
    songsMapping[uuid] = managedObject.objectID
    return uuid
}
```

Add a New Cache Node

Adding a new cache node is similar to what we did earlier when we loaded data from the file, but in the opposite direction – from the context down to the store.

To do that, we need to implement the following:

```
override func newCacheNode(for managedObject: NSManagedObject)
-> NSAtomicStoreCacheNode {
    let cacheNode = NSAtomicStoreCacheNode(objectID:
    managedObject.objectID)
    // fill with data from the managed object
    return cacheNode
}
```

Now, even though the implementation looks obvious, there is a small catch: relationships.

If we insert a new object with relationships, we need to make sure that when we create a new cache node, **we take care of all the wiring and linking**.

One of the things that can help us is the **mapping** that we did between the reference objects and the objectIDs.

Once we have an objectID, all we need to do is to retrieve its cache node (if exists in our memory) and perform the relevant connection:

```
if let albumNode = self.cacheNode(for: albumObjectID) {
        cacheNode.setValue(albumNode, forKey: "album")
} else {
        // create a new album cache node from data.
}
```

NSAtomicStore has a function called cacheNode(for objectID: NSManagedObjectID) that can help us get a cache node by objectID, and we need to use it to connect everything we need.

Saving

The final step would be to update our local file with all the new changes.

Core Data calls the store's save method, and we should implement it in our subclass:

```
override func save() throws {}
```

But what is the right way to do that?

There are several ways to implement that, and it depends on how you choose to track your data.

One way would be to take the brute-force approach. We have a map with all the objectIDs, so we can generate cache nodes for all of them and, from the cache nodes, create the data that we can save for our CSV file.

That may be the most reliable and simple way of saving our data back to the file, but it's not the most elegant approach.

Another way would be to keep the data created when we loaded the CSV file and update it with the changes every time we update or insert a new cache node.

Once we need to save the data back to the file, we have it already updated with all the changes.

Remember that you don't need to worry about handling multiple contexts – this is the Core Data container's job. Saving to the store and inserting new cache nodes only happens when the app requests to save the data locally.

Updating and Deleting

Just like adding a new cache node, updating and deleting require implementing additional methods.

For updating a node, we need to implement the following:

```
override func updateCacheNode(_ node: NSAtomicStoreCacheNode,
from managedObject: NSManagedObject) {

    }
```

Notice that NSAtomicStore makes life easier for you – it already gives you the node and the managed object.

Now that is a good time to reuse the code from the newCacheNode function and consolidate it in one place.

Removing cache nodes is done similarly – Core Data calls the willRemoveCacheNodes method just before the cache nodes are removed from the store.

This is where we need to remove the corresponding data and relationships.

NSIncrementalStore

Unlike `NSAtomicStore`, `NSIncrementalStore` aims to solve other situations where you can't hold the store in memory and need to load the data only when required.

There are two primary use cases for that: when the data store is too big to hold in memory and when the data is not saved on the device and you can fetch it upon request only, like a web service.

But first, let's talk about how we build an `NSIncrementalStore` of our own.

I think that the most important thing to understand is the fact that we have much more control and therefore much more responsibility.

Implementing `NSAtomicStore` was simple. All we had to do was fetch all our records, connect them to a reference ID, and fill cache nodes.

In `NSIncrementalStore,` we have two primary jobs:

- We need to handle all the store operations ourselves, such as fetching, saving, and deleting.

- We need to manage faulting. Remember, it's incremental, and we load only what we need.

Let's get to work.

Loading the Store

Incremental stores usually work with a local file (in many cases, it's a SQLite file) and need to make sure the file is in the correct location (and if not, create it).

The `loadMetaData()` method is the place where we need to handle that:

```swift
override func loadMetadata() throws {
```

```
    if let dir = FileManager.default.urls(for:
    .documentDirectory,
                                in: .userDomainMask).first {
        let path = dir.appendingPathComponent("myMusic.
        sqlite")
        if !FileManager.default.fileExists(atPath: path) {
            // create the store
        }
    }
}
```

This is also the place for doing other two things:

  – **Check** if the file is **corrupted** and throw an error.

  – **Load basic data** from the store (optional).

Let's elaborate on what "loading basic data" means.

Indeed, incremental stores are not like atomic stores – we don't load **all the data** into memory.

But it doesn't mean we can't load any data at all.

For example, if we have an enormous store of songs, we can load their IDs into memory, making it easier for us to fetch additional data when needed.

Fetching something like "headers" can ease our implementation, and as a bonus, it's a great way to make sure our file is not corrupted and in the correct format.

Execute Store Requests

To make our incremental store work properly, the first thing we need to handle is store requests from our context – remember, the context is our "client" now that we are a store.

In incremental stores we need to implement the following method:

```
override func execute(_ request: NSPersistentStoreRequest, with
context: NSManagedObjectContext?) throws -> Any
```

The execute() function has two parameters: the store request itself
(we'll talk about it in a minute) and the relevant context.

This function handles fetch requests, saving, and even batch actions.

NSPersistentStoreRequest

The NSPersistentStoreRequest instance in the execute() method
signature encapsulates all the necessary information to perform what the
context requests us to do.

First, we need to understand what type of request we have. Therefore,
we need to check the requestType property of the instance:

```
override func execute(_ request: NSPersistentStoreRequest, with
context: NSManagedObjectContext?) throws -> Any {
    if request.requestType == .fetchRequestType {
        // performing fetching
    }
    return []
}
```

Fetching

When the requestType property equals fetchRequestType, we know the
context is trying to perform **a fetch request**.

In this case, we can cast it to a fetch request and check what entity is
being requested:

```
if request.requestType == .fetchRequestType {
    if let fetchRequest = request as?
    NSFetchRequest<NSManagedObject> {
```

```
if fetchRequest.entityName == "Song" {
    // fetching data from our backing store
  }
 }
}
```

Now that we have the entity name, we can create our songs based on the fetch request:

```
if fetchRequest.entityName == "Song" {
    let songsIDs = self.getSongsIds(byRequest: fetchRequest)
    var songs : [NSManagedObject] = []
    for songID in songsIDs {
        let objectID = self.newObjectID(for:
        fetchRequest.entity!, referenceObject: songID)
          if let song = context?.object(with: objectID) {
              songs.append(song)
              }
          }
          return songs
      }
```

Let's talk about the preceding code.

First, we have a particular function called getSongsIds(byRequest:). We need to write this function, and it needs to retrieve song IDs from our backing store according to the fetch request it receives.

The fetch request contains all the information we need, including a predicate and sort descriptors.

This is the most complicated work you need to do here – how to use the predicate and sort descriptor you've got to perform a request to your CSV or SQLite file?

My tip here is that you don't need to cover all the possible use cases of predicates and sorting.

While you are building your app and adding more and more fetch requests, analyze the fetch request **according to your needs** and add the relevant code as you go. Don't try to replicate SQLite-based incremental stores entirely – this is not the goal of building an incremental store.

Once we have all the song IDs, we can perform a for loop and create a managed object for each one of them.

Notice we don't just initialize a new managed object in every loop iteration – we first generate an objectID derived from the entity description and the songID. **Only then** do we retrieve a managed object from the context.

If the context already has a managed object with this objectID, it will return the existing one.

The songID is the reference object and unique identifier for our objects. Attaching it to the objectID is our store's way to register our records from the backing store.

Another thing you might have noticed is that we don't fill our songs with data at all – that's because we initialize only faulted objects. Remember that Core Data feature?

Faulting lets us optimize our requests and load additional data only on requests. We'll cover faulting soon!

Saving

Going back to the start of the execute() function, as I mentioned, this function handles not just fetching **but also saving**.

But what exactly is a "saving" store request?

Well, "saving" means inserting, updating, and deleting objects.

To handle saving requests, we first need to check the request type and compare it to saveRequestType.

The next step would be casting the fetch request to NSSaveChangesRequest.

Yes, the execute() function uses polymorphism here – it sometimes can be a fetch request and sometimes a save request.

Like the fetch request, the save request also **encapsulates all the information needed** to save the new data to your store.

The NSSaveChangesRequest has three properties:

- insertedObjects

- updatedObjects

- deletedObjects

Each of them is an array containing the list of objects being requested to save.

What are these objects? Well, in this case, the objects are actually NSManagedObject. If you cast them to Song (for example), you will be able to retrieve all the information needed for saving it in your backing store.

Let's see the saving request in action:

```
if request.requestType == .saveRequestType {
        let saveRequest = request as! NSSaveChangesRequest
        for newObject in saveRequest.insertedObjects! {
                if let song = newObject as? Song {
                        try addNewSongToBackingStore(song: song)
                }
        }
}
```

ObjectID

Now, take a moment, read the preceding code, and think if something is missing.

Hint: Look at the code we wrote earlier when we loaded all the data from the backing store and registered it to the incremental store.

Are you there yet?

We **need to map the objectID to its reference value** ("songID" in this case). Remember that?

The reason it doesn't happen in the execute() function is that, as you probably know, new objects added to Core Data have a temporary objectID. They get their permanent objectID only after the saving operation is completed.

This is also the time where Core Data will ask you to **obtain a permanent objectID**, using the function obtainPermanentIDs():

```
override func obtainPermanentIDs(for array: [NSManagedObject])
throws -> [NSManagedObjectID] {
        var objectIDs = [NSManagedObjectID]()
        for object in array {
            if let song = object as? Song {
                let referenceID = song.songID
                let objectID = self.newObjectID(for: song.
                entity, referenceObject: referenceID)
                objectIDs.append(objectID)
            }
        }
        return objectIDs
    }
```

The obtainPermanentIDs function passes a list of new objects and requires returning a list of corresponding object IDs.

I think that the implementation should already be familiar to you by now.

obtainPermanentIDs is another excellent example of how learning about NSIncrementalStore reveals how Core Data works under the hood. Suddenly, many things become more evident.

But there is one more piece missing to the puzzle, and that's **faulting**.

Faulting

Remember when we fetched objects but didn't fetch their data and I told you we'd talk about faulting soon? These objects were like "ghosts," empty objects.

When the "user" (the user is actually the app itself) calls song.name, we need to go and fetch the name if required.

Fortunately, NSIncrementalStore helps us with managing that area very well.

We only need to implement one more function, and that's newValuesForObject.

This function gets called when the store needs to fulfill an object with information from the store.

Just like atomic stores, we don't fill the managed object ourselves – we use a node here, NSIncrementalStoreNode to be precise:

```
override func newValuesForObject(with objectID:
NSManagedObjectID, with context: NSManagedObjectContext)
throws -> NSIncrementalStoreNode {
        guard let songID = self.referenceObject(for: objectID)
        as? String else {
            throw MyIncrementalStoreError.noReferenceID
        }

        let data = getValuesFromBackingStore(forSongID: songID)
        let version = getVersion(forSongID: songID) + 1
        let node = NSIncrementalStoreNode(objectID: objectID,
        withValues: data, version: version)
        updateVersion(forSongsID: songID, version: version)
        return node
}
```

The code is straightforward except for one thing – the version (I marked that in bold).

When we create the NSIncrementalStoreNode, we need to provide a version that should be incremented every time the node is created.

The "version" helps merge conflicts and should be saved persistently – a specific version for a row. In the preceding example, I read the version from the disk and saved it back – to maintain it for future fetches.

NSIncrementalStore keeps track of faulted objects for us – and this is basically the hard work that needs to be done.

What about relationships?

For relationships, we have an additional method we need to override:

```
func newValue(forRelationship relationship:
NSRelationshipDescription, forObjectWith objectID:
NSManagedObjectID, with context: NSManagedObjectContext?)
throws -> Any
```

Even though it looks scary, relationship faulting is superficial. All we need to do is to analyze what the destination entity is and return its NSManagedObjectID (or IDs in case of a to-many relationship).

Look at the following implementation:

```
override func newValue(forRelationship relationship:
NSRelationshipDescription, forObjectWith objectID:
NSManagedObjectID, with context: NSManagedObjectContext?)
throws -> Any {
        let songID = self.referenceObject(for: objectID)
        as! String
        guard let destDescription = relationship.
        destinationEntity else {
            throw MyIncrementalStoreError.noEntitiyDescription
        }
        if destDescription.name == "Album" {
```

```
        let albumID = self.getAlbumID(forSongID: songID)
        let albumObjectID = self.newObjectID(for:
        destDescription, referenceObject: albumID)
        return albumObjectID
    }

    if destDescription.name == "Composer" {
        if relationship.isToMany {
            var objectIDs = Set<NSManagedObjectID>()
            let composerIDs = getComposerIDs
            (fromSongID: songID)
            for composerID in composerIDs {
                let composerObjectID = self.
                newObjectID(for: destDescription,
                referenceObject: composerID)
                objectIDs.insert(composerObjectID)
            }
            return objectIDs
        }
    }

    throw MyIncrementalStoreError.noEntitiyDescription
}
```

I handled two relationships in the preceding example – one for Album
(to-one) and one for Composer (to-many).

And if you ask yourself where the object data is, you should know the
answer by now. If Core Data needs it, it will ask the data by calling the
newValuesForObject() function. Your job is just to implement it.

Web Services

Here's a section that I mentioned early, and it probably still sounds weird to you. Because the incremental store is incremental, a possible use case for implementing such a store is to connect the store directly to your backend API.

Think of it for a second – we have a perfectly excellent object graph framework with predicates, sorting, and caching mechanisms.

You are using that mechanism for your app anyway. Why do you "care" if the data is received from your local or remote storage?

That's part of the beauty of Core Data. As I said more than once, Core Data **is not a SQLite wrapper**. It's much more than that.

This is where you manage your entities, and the option of binding it directly to your server may be a great approach.

The primary problem with connecting our store to a server is that calling an HTTP request is a **time-consuming operation** and may take a few seconds to return.

All the steps inside your store must be synchronized – Core Data stores don't support async operations.

Executing a Core Data request from the app should conclude that fact and perform on a background thread, considering all the Core Data background operation constraints that we are already aware of.

Summary

Implementing incremental and atomic stores is one of the fascinating subjects to learn when diving into Core Data, not because of what you can do with it but rather what you can learn from it.

It's an excellent opportunity to switch your position in iOS development and think as a framework maker for a second.

We've learned how to create atomic and incremental stores and how they can serve us by connecting our store directly to our back end.

Now is the time to see how Core Data can connect to more iOS features.

CHAPTER 12

Core Data and the World

> *Sometimes it pays to stay in bed on Monday, rather than spending the rest of the week debugging Monday's code.*
>
> —Dan Salomon

In the previous chapter, we learned how to create our own custom store type. We touched on Core Data's most profound internal aspects and learned closely about how everything is connected.

Now, we will do the opposite and learn how Core Data can communicate with the outside world and be shared with humankind.

In this chapter, you will learn

- How to integrate Core Data with Spotlight

- How to share our store with other apps and extensions we might have

- How to sync Core Data with iCloud using the CloudKit framework

© Avi Tsadok 2022
A. Tsadok, *Unleash Core Data*, https://doi.org/10.1007/978-1-4842-8211-3_12

Integrate with Spotlight

One of the best things about working with Core Data is that Core Data is a **homemade framework**.

Not only does Xcode work well with Core Data and have many built-in tools to support it but it also works amazingly with other built-in frameworks.

One of these frameworks is Spotlight.

A Few Words About Spotlight

You probably bumped into the term **Spotlight** more than once. Spotlight is Apple's search engine used in macOS and iOS.

To provide app developers the option to index their content to Spotlight, Apple created `Core Spotlight` – a framework that enables you to decide what items will be indexed and how.

How do we index our data?

In most cases, it's the developer's responsibility to handle the Spotlight index. For each item we want to index, we do something called `CSSearchableItem` and append it to the Spotlight index. `CSSearchableItem` represents an item that will appear in Spotlight search results.

But our job doesn't end here. We also need to **maintain these indexes overtime**. App content is dynamic and often changes – it gets deleted or renamed, and new content is being created overtime.

That's where the integration between Core Data and Core Spotlight comes in handy.

Core Data and Core Spotlight

To overcome the hassle of maintaining the app data updated in Spotlight results, the integration between Core Data and Core Spotlight takes care of most of the work for us.

Let's start with the requirements for such integration:

- First, we need to tell Core Data **what entities and attributes** need to be indexed.

- We need to make sure this integration **tracks every change** in our store so that the index will be updated constantly.

- We need to **convert** managed objects to search items so that Spotlight can index and display them correctly.

I know I said that the integration is ready almost out of the box, and then I presented three steps, but believe me describing these steps takes more time than implementing them!

Let's start with the first one – define the entities supposed to be indexed in Core Spotlight.

"Index in Spotlight"

Applications that use Core Data may contain many objects from many different entities. Because of **efficiency** reasons, we don't want Core Spotlight to index all our entities.

In fact, Apple specifies that Core Spotlight is efficient with indexes that have no more than a few thousand records.

So, naturally, we need to define precisely what objects and attributes we want Core Spotlight to index.

To do that, we will open our data model in Xcode and select the entity and attribute we want to index.

In the data model inspector, you can find an advanced setting named "Index in Spotlight" (see Figure 12-1).

Figure 12-1. *"Index in Spotlight" setting*

Marking the desired attribute signals Core Spotlight what attributes and entities it needs to index.

Like any other index, this is a tradeoff between speed and space. Marking a specific attribute **doesn't mean you can't search** other attributes as well.

And what about versioning? Do we need to create a new data model version to use this checkbox?

The good news is that you can use this feature without creating a new data model version. The bad news is that you didn't know this option existed until now…

That step was easy! The next step requires a little bit more work, and that's **turning on history tracking**.

Persistent History Tracking

Earlier, we said that in order to create our own index for searching, we need to respond to any changes we have in our store and update our index accordingly.

Core Data has the option to preserve transaction logs no matter their source. For example, changes to our data might occur due to data migrations, an extension (such as widget) action, or updates that arrive from iCloud.

This option of saving all the change history is not enabled by default, and we need to turn it on.

We do that by configuring the persistent container:

```
let description = NSPersistentStoreDescription(url:(container.
persistentStoreDescriptions.first?.url)!)
description.type = NSSQLiteStoreType
description.setOption(true as NSNumber, forKey:
NSPersistentHistoryTrackingKey)
container.persistentStoreDescriptions = [description]
```

Notice something interesting in the preceding code – we set the description type to NSSQLiteStoreType. One of the Spotlight integration requirements is for the **data store to be SQLite based**.

In most cases, that will be okay – the in-memory store is not relevant to Spotlight integration, and most of the apps use SQLite anyway, but that is just something you need to keep in mind, especially after what we've learned in the previous chapter – how to build your own custom store.

Create a Core Spotlight Delegate

We barely did something, and we are almost done with the integration. Actual coding starts now!

Our final step is to create a Core Spotlight Delegate and start the actual index.

A Core Spotlight Delegate is an instance that handles the **mapping** between managed objects and Spotlight search attributes.

To create a Core Spotlight Delegate, we need to subclass NSCoreDataCoreSpotlightDelegate and override some methods to define the mapping.

Let's see an example:

```
import Foundation
import CoreData
import CoreSpotlight

class SongSpotlightDelegate: NSCoreDataCoreSpotlightDelegate {

    override func domainIdentifier() -> String {
        return "com.myMusicApp.www"
    }

    override func indexName() -> String? {
        return "songs-index"
    }

    override func attributeSet(for object: NSManagedObject)
    -> CSSearchableItemAttributeSet? {

        guard let song = object as? Song else {return nil}

        let attributeSet = CSSearchableItemAttributeSet
        (contentType: .text)
        attributeSet.displayName = song.name
        attributeSet.textContent = song.album?.title ?? ""
        return attributeSet

    }
}
```

The SongSpotlightDelegate class is a small but efficient one. We override three functions.

The first is the domain identifier, which is basically the app bundle identifier.

In the indexName() function, we will return the index name as it appears in debugging tools and the console.

The important and interesting function we need to override is `attributeSet(for object:)`.

This function gets a managed object and returns `CSSearchableItemAttributeSet` if relevant.

One thing to notice here is that you **can't create multiple delegates** in a single store.

It means that you should do it here in this function for any mapping you want to do.

If you need to map multiple entities, it is recommended you separate that logic to different files and classes and call them from that function. Remember, it is always better to create more separations instead of having a bloated function.

Our next step will be creating the delegate instance and connecting it to our container.

To do that, we will write the following method:

```
private func configureContainer(desc:
NSPersistentStoreDescription, container:
NSPersistentContainer) {
        let coordiantor = container.persistentStoreCoordinator
        self.spotlightIndexer = SongSpotlightDelegate(forStore
        With: desc, coordinator: coordiantor)
        self.spotlightIndexer?.startSpotlightIndexing()
    }
```

The function gets the persistent description and the persistent container as parameters and initializes a new `SongSpotlightDelegate` instance to start the indexing.

This instance **should be kept alive all the time** – that's why we need to keep it as an instance variable (in this case, in our App Delegate).

Also, notice the call for `startSpotlightIndexing()` – **that's an async operation**, so you don't need to perform it on a background thread and worry it might block the main thread.

The importance of this function is its timing. The startSpotlightIndexing() function must be called **after** the store finished being loaded for an obvious reason – if the store hasn't been loaded yet, the delegate has nothing to index yet.

So our next task will be to synchronize the delegate creation and indexing with store loading:

```
container.loadPersistentStores(completionHandler: {
(storeDescription, error) in
                if let error = error as NSError? {
                fatalError("Unresolved error \(error), \(error.
                userInfo)")
        }

        self.configureContainer(desc: description,
        container: container)
    })
```

Now, run your project and have a look at your console:

```
CoreData: debug: NSCoreDataCoreSpotlightDelegate
initializing support for store description for
<NSPersistentStoreDescription: 0x600002f2e6a0>
CoreData: debug: Allowing indexing request (1).
CoreData: debug: NSCoreDataCoreSpotlightDelegate finished
initialization for persistent store for 91621CBD-2B24-40B9-
BC83-1B7EB50ADA32
CoreData: debug: Do *not* need additional indexing
operation (0).
```

Core Data sends you helpful information about your Spotlight indexing, and that's a good signal that things are working correctly.

Delete the Indexing

One important thing to remember is that the Spotlight indexing is not really bound to your Core Data store.

The Spotlight Index Delegate is smart enough to index changes that you perform in your store, but there are cases where you need to completely remove the index if it's not relevant anymore.

One example would be "log-out" – when the user logs out from your store, your index is no longer relevant. Apart from clearing your local store, you also need to remove your Spotlight index.

Clearing your index is also part of the Core Spotlight Delegate:

```
private func clearSpotlightIndex() {
                    self.spotlightIndexer?.deleteSpotlight
                    Index(completionHandler: { error in
        if let error = error {
            NSLog("Error Cleaning Index: %@", error.
            localizedDescription)
        }
    })
}
```

Small Note About Privacy

In general, Spotlight–Core Data integration is simple and straightforward. But there is something you should be aware of, and that's **privacy and security**.

Whenever we share our data to other extensions or, in the case of Spotlight, let other services index our data, we expose data outside our app.

There are cases where such exposure is legit and obvious, for example, when building a music app.

But when dealing with sensitive data, that could be a problem. A payment or a calendar app is a good example.

Like many other aspects of data handling, this is another issue you should consider.

Share the Core Data Store with App Extensions

Spotlight integration is not the only place where your app data is relevant outside your app.

App extensions are a perfect example for sharing your data, for example, home widgets, sharing extensions, and more.

But the same concerns I raised are relevant here as well.

iOS prevents apps from accessing other apps' resources and data, and the same applies to extensions and apps.

App Container

When apps and extensions are from the same developer, Apple allows you to create a shared folder called Container (Figure 12-2).

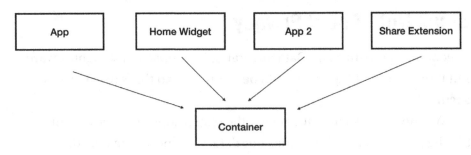

Figure 12-2. *The Container folder*

In this way, app developers can share data between their app and its extensions and even between one app and another.

So what we want to do now is to locate the Core Data persistent store inside that container.

Our first step will be to set up the container.

App Group

First, let's meet a new term – *app group.*

An app group allows different products (extensions, apps, etc.) from the same developer to share data and communicate.

Your project needs to support **at least one app group to share a resource between the different products**. In big projects with several teams, we may find multiple app groups.

iOS creates a shared container for each app group (see Figure 12-3).

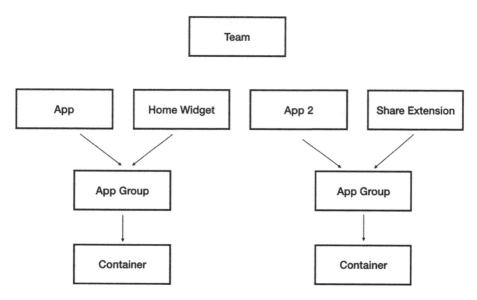

Figure 12-3. *App groups and containers*

The way app groups and containers work provides bigger teams the flexibility to create different containers for different needs.

Adding the App Group in Xcode

Adding a new app group has one but necessary step.

Besides adding the capability to your project, it creates entitlement and syncs it to your Apple Developer Portal.

To add the new app group to your project, open Xcode, go to your project, and tap on your app target.

Now, tap on the "Signing & Capabilities" tab (Figure 12-4).

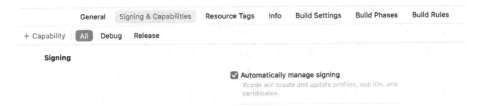

Figure 12-4. *"Signing & Capabilities" tab*

Add a new capability named "App Groups" (Figure 12-5).

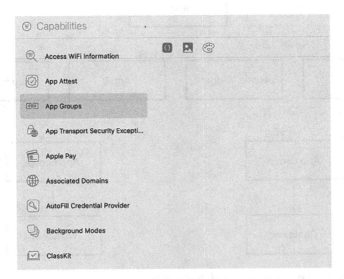

Figure 12-5. *"App Groups" capability*

After adding the new "App Groups" capability, scroll the list of capabilities and locate it. Add a new app group and provide its name (Figure 12-6).

Figure 12-6. *The new app group*

Remember to do that step **for all the targets** supposed to access the shared container.

Working with the New Container Folder

As I said earlier, creating a new app group also creates a shared container that can be used across your products.

Therefore, our next step will be **setting the store local URL** to be inside that shared container.

To get the shared container URL, we can use the iOS File Manager containerURL method:

```
if let sharedURL = FileManager.default.containerURL(forSecurity
ApplicationGroupIdentifier: "group.unleashCoreData") {

        }
```

Because our app can support multiple app groups, we need to pass the app group identifier we created earlier.

Our full code is supposed to look like this:

```
let container = NSPersistentContainer(name: "MyDataModel")
        if let sharedURL = FileManager.default.containerU
        RL(forSecurityApplicationGroupIdentifier: "group.
        unleashCoreData") {
```

```
    let storeURL = sharedURL.
    appendingPathComponent("file.sqlite")
    let storeDescription = NSPersistentStoreDescription
    (url: storeURL)
    container.persistentStoreDescriptions =
    [storeDescription]
}
```

You should already be familiar with the rest of the code – adding the file name, creating a store description, and adding it to the container.

To clear things up, let's see how our app architecture works with the new container (Figure 12-7).

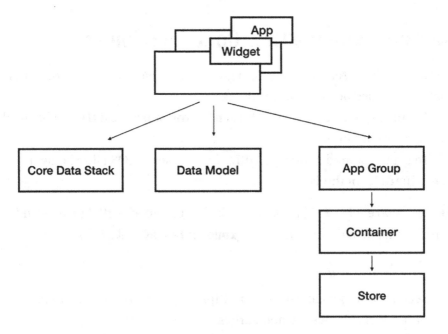

Figure 12-7. *App architecture using the shared container*

There's a reason for what I showed you in Figure 12-7 – the data store is not the only thing we share.

All products that need access to your data store need to

– Have **access to the data model** so that they can load the store correctly.

– Share the **same Core Data initialization code**, so they will be able to load the same store URL.

Because of the reasons I mentioned previously, Figure 12-7 suggests that the data model and the Core Data stack need to be shared across your products.

Now, this is just a suggestion. We can duplicate the data model (don't do it!) or use other design patterns to share the Core Data store besides using the same Core Data stack.

For example, we can **extract the store URL to a separate class** and share it across our targets.

In general, good separation of concerns provides flexibility, and that's also the case here.

Adding an Extension to an Existing App

The code I showed you earlier might be nice in fairy tales and tutorials you can find across the Web, but the reality is slightly different.

In real life, most development teams start with an app, and only after it has a store they add an extension.

And in the use case of an extension (which is more common), the problem is that we already have a store, and it's not located in the shared container but the app library folder.

The solution is, of course, moving the store file from the app library to the new shared folder.

But how?

Why Not Use File Manager?

Our first instinct is "Okay, we have the original file location and the new location. Why not just use NSFileManager to change file location?"

That's one of the cases where I don't recommend you to "follow your instincts."

Moving the store using a direct NSFileManager operation has two problems.

First, it doesn't notify Core Data that the store location **has been updated** so that Core Data can work properly.

Second, who told us that the Core Data store is a single file? SQLite, for example, **uses two additional files** to manage transactions – SHM and WAL files.

WAL files, for example, are used to contain transactions that haven't yet been added to the main data store, and SHM files contain shared data among processes.

These are internal files used by SQLite and Core Data, so moving only the main file may cause some data loss we really don't want.

Use the migratePersistentStore Method

You already know me – I never bring up a problem without showing you a solution.

Lucky us, Core Data has **a dedicated function** to solve that issue, and that's migratePersistentStore:

```
if let store = container.persistentStoreCoordinator.
persistentStore(for: oldURL)         {
    do {
        _ = try container.persistentStoreCoordinator.
        migratePersistentStore(store, to: sharedURL,
        options: nil, type: .sqlite)
    } catch let error {
```

```
        print("error moving store: \(error.
        localizedDescription)")
    }
}
```

Some things to notice here: Migrating your store does not move the store files **but copies them**, and that's important.

First, it means that the operation might take time to complete.

But it also means that if we want it to be a one-time action, we need to think about the pre-check condition.

If we do something like

```
if oldStoreExists {
    migrateToNewLocation()
}
```

our migration will constantly run because the "old" store is always there – there's no stopping condition. We need to remove the old store or change our condition to

```
if !newStoreExists {
    migrateToNewLocation()
}
```

To summarize this part, migrating the store to a new location is a sensitive operation; any failure may be devastating.

Consider every move carefully, and if possible, create an app group once you have a chance to make things simpler in the future.

For example, if you build an app from scratch, add an app group from the beginning to avoid migrating in the future.

Core Data and CloudKit

At the beginning of the chapter, we've learned how to expose Core Data to the world by integrating it with Spotlight.

Later, we learned how to expose Core Data to other products we might have, such as widgets and share extensions.

Now it's time to share Core Data not only with the system and our products but also with **other devices the user might have**.

If you are not familiar with CloudKit, it's a framework that aims to share data across user devices using iCloud.

CloudKit can share data such as key-value and documents, but it can also share data records, represented by the class CKRecord.

Two more terms related to CKRecord are Schema (that defines the different models and their relationships) and CDRecordZone (that represents the store where the scheme and the records are saved).

If that reminds you of something, you are not wrong.

CKRecord is equivalent to NSManagedObject, Scheme is equivalent to NSManagedObjectModel, and CDRecordZone is equivalent to NSPersistentStore.

Based on that, it's just natural for Apple to create a seamless integration between Core Data and CloudKit, to provide an easy way for developers to share their data.

Set Up CloudKit

Setting up CloudKit is simple and has nothing to do with Core Data.

Our first step will be adding the iCloud capability and enabling the CloudKit service (Figure 12-8).

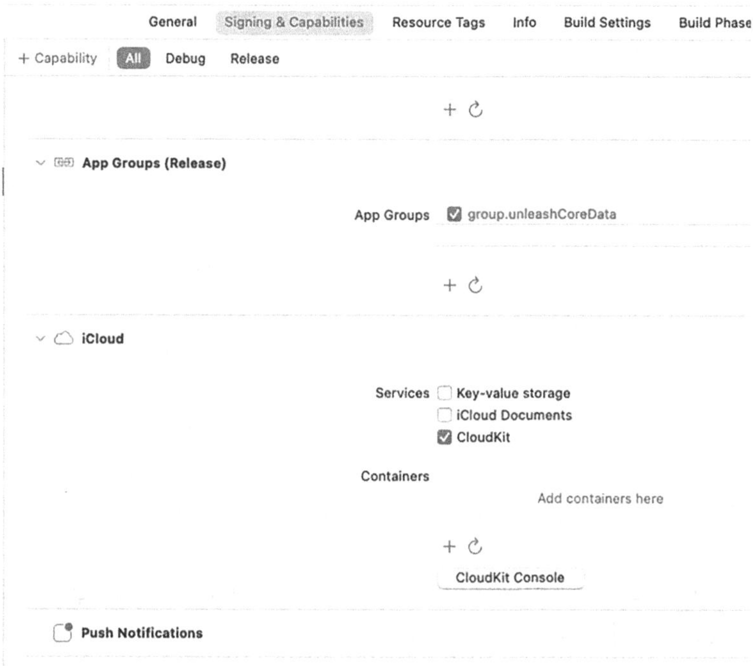

Figure 12-8. *Enable the CloudKit service*

Notice that enabling the CloudKit service also adds the Push Notification capability.

Our second (and final!) step will be adding the "Background Modes" capability and enabling the Remote Notifications mode (Figure 12-9).

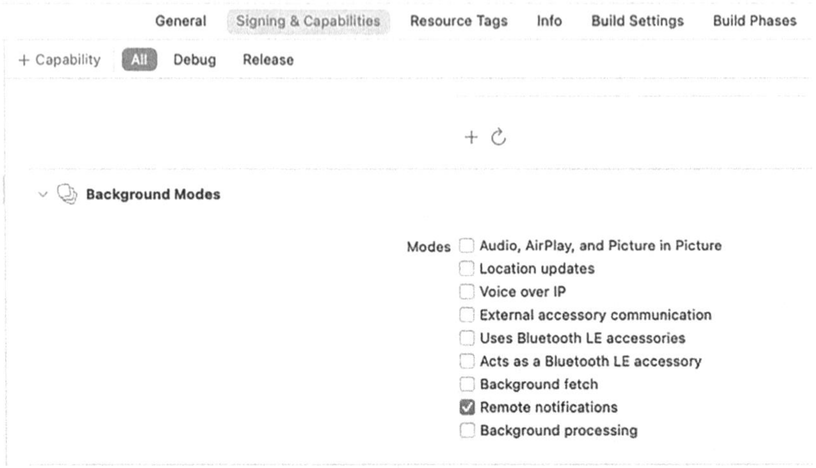

Figure 12-9. Enabling the Remote Notifications mode

Push notifications are essential for our Core Data store to **get updates from iCloud** when your app is not active.

Why did I mention that this is the last step? Don't we need to register to remote notifications, sync the device token, and observe incoming notifications?

One of the nicest things about CloudKit is that the framework takes care of everything, including responding to silent push notifications for you!

You can continue implementing the integration. Not much left.

The Integration

Let's talk about the integration for a second.

Every change we do on our local store is **being translated** to CKRecord and pushed to iCloud by CloudKit.

At this stage, iCloud **sends a (silent) push notification** to the other devices and notifies them something has changed.

The CloudKit framework on the other device receives the change, gets the CKRecord, and **translates it back** to NSManagedObject.

Remember we talked about history tracking and changes being received by external products? That's one of the cases.

Persistent history tracking allows CloudKit to look back at the changes made and make sure to update iCloud accordingly.

As you can see, almost nothing is changing in the way we work with Core Data, while the CloudKit framework does all the heavy sync code.

Data Model Limitations

Because our data needs to be synced and be compatible with the way iCloud stores the data in its container, there **are a couple of limitations** in the data model you should be aware of.

Some of them are as follows:

- The Deny rule is not supported in relationships.

- Relationships must have an inverse.

- Relationships must be optional.

Note   It is recommended to be updated with the Apple Developer site about all the different limitations.

Most limitations are not deal-breakers, and you can ideally overcome them. If some of them are important for your flow, you can always take care of the functionality in your code.

NSPersistentCloudKitContainer

After we added support for CloudKit and made sure our data model is CloudKit-ready, we need to perform small changes to how we set up our Core Data stack.

Lucky us, Apple has made the integration super easy for us.

Let's look back at our container:

```
let container = NSPersistentContainer(name: "MyDataModel")
```

Other than simplifying the creation of the persistent store and the main context, NSPersistentContainer also handles the integrations between the different Core Data stack layers (if you don't know what I'm talking about, go back to the beginning of the book).

The container is the exact place where we need to make a change to integrate Core Data with CloudKit.

The primary change we need to do is to **replace** the NSPersistentContainer class with its subclass, NSPersistentCloudKitContainer:

```
let container = NSPersistentCloudKitContainer (name:
"MyDataModel")
```

NSPersistentCloudKitContainer makes sure that your local store is **constantly mirrored** to the user's CloudKit private database.

Another step we need to do is make sure changes from iCloud are merged in runtime and automaticallyMergesChangesFromParent is set to true:

```
let viewContext = persistentContainer.viewContextviewContext.
automaticallyMergesChangesFromParent = true
```

And that's it. You're there!

Add CloudKit to an Existing App

Setting up CloudKit integration looks so easy and simple when we build an app from scratch.

What do we do when we have an already existing store?

Well, adding support to an existing store may be a little tricky.

There are a couple of things you should be aware of – let's detail them.

Store Location

NSPersistentCloudKitContainer works with stores in their "default" location. If you don't change the store URL when creating a container, everything will be fine when moving to the CloudKit container.

But, if your store was **created in a different location**, you will need to migrate it to support CloudKit.

What are the cases where it can happen? For example, if you started to implement Core Data back in the old days **before iOS 10**. In this case, the Core Data store was created in the Documents folder and not in the "Library" folder like in the case of the container.

When that happens, you first need to check if the default location contains a store (using FileManager) and, if not, migrate the old store to the new location using migratePersistentStore.

Make Existing Data Sync to iCloud

That one is a pain point for many developers who implemented a CloudKit integration and wondered why their existing data didn't sync.

Let's clarify how CloudKit integration works. The CloudKit framework observes changes and transactions that happen in your store. For example, adding a new record is considered a **change** and therefore synced to iCloud. The same goes for renaming/setting a value or deleting an object.

But what happens to existing, "untouched" (yet!) records?

Well, if we don't modify these records, CloudKit won't "see" them and, as a result, won't sync them to iCloud.

That's a massive deal to an app developer who wants to add CloudKit support to its app, and it's a problem Apple hasn't solved (yet!).

Some workarounds are not perfect but can work. Let's list them.

Make Sure Persistent History Tracking Is Enabled

The first solution was already mentioned at the beginning of this chapter, and that's **enabling persistent history tracking**.

What persistent history tracking does is create a transaction log of the changes we do in our store.

Every record in this log will be synced to iCloud once you move to CloudKit integration.

But what it also means is that records that were last changed **before you enabled persistent history tracking** won't sync to iCloud, so consider that.

In most cases, this is a recommended step, but as a solution, it does not fulfill your requirements for the problem.

Modify All Your Records

The previous solution of persistent history tracking is probably an "Apple-style" solution, but we already saw it's not perfect.

Another approach is the "brute-force" solution, and that's **modifying all the records** in your store to make them sync.

For example, you can add a Bool attribute to all of them and set it to true.

If you feel deep inside you that this solution is wrong and you are not comfortable with it, that's perfectly understood.

But it's a workaround that will make all of your data sync to CloudKit.

Combining that with persistent history tracking is a truly robust solution to the problem.

Notice that this action should happen only once when upgrading to CloudKit.

Recreate Objects

If you don't want to add an attribute to your objects and "dirty" them, I have another solution for you – recreate all your objects.

Open a new private context, iterate all your objects, and create them again. Then, delete the old objects.

That will upload all of them to iCloud.

It's another brute-force solution, but it's much cleaner this time.

None of the preceding solutions are perfect, but they may be a small price to pay for a free and simple cloud store service for your app.

Summary

You store can live outside your app, while the primary concerns are privacy, security, and consistent data.

Remember to be careful in what you do! Be responsible because your user data is the most critical thing in your app.

In this chapter, we learned

- How to integrate our store with Spotlight

- How to share our store with different extensions and apps

- How to sync our store data to iCloud

CHAPTER 13

What's Next?

Computers are incredibly fast, accurate, and stupid. Human beings are incredibly slow, inaccurate, and brilliant. Together they are powerful beyond imagination.

—Albert Einstein

What Have We Learned Till Now?

It was a long journey!

And that's obvious – Core Data not only is an extensive framework but also represents the **data layer**, and as a result, it plays a significant role in your app architecture.

This book is built upon three parts – **the basics** (how to set up an excellent Core Data infrastructure), **implementation** (performances, predicates, concurrency), and **advanced features** (custom data stores, SwiftUI, and integrations).

But there is so much left we haven't covered at all, for example:

- – Testing

- – Swift Package Manager integrations

- – Data model configurations

- – Parent entities

A. Tsadok, *Unleash Core Data*, https://doi.org/10.1007/978-1-4842-8211-3_13

These are just a tiny part of what's left, and the way I see it, it is okay.

As I said in one of the chapters, the book's primary goal is **not** to be massive documentation or a huge folder of tutorials.

Its goal is to unleash the power of Core Data for those who are afraid to start or were frustrated in the past with how they worked with Core Data.

How to Start?

I think that's the tricky question.

I would divide the answer into three parts:

- Understand your needs (is Core Data even relevant for you?).

- Design your data model (based on the existing app).

- Implement Core Data to an existing project.

Understand Your Needs

Using Core Data is suitable for many projects, but not **all** of them. You should analyze your requirements from your data layer and conclude your decision.

Some questions you can ask yourself are

- What types of data are you planning to store?

- What amount of data are you planning to hold?

- What are the relationships between your entities?

- What kinds of queries are you planning to perform?

- Do you need to share your database with other platforms?

- What is the link between your data and the UI?

The preceding questions can assist you in understanding what your needs are.

For example, if you need to import many objects from the same entities and perform standard search queries, Core Data may not be the best solution for you.

Core Data can perform the task efficiently, but its strengths are laid in different aspects.

For example, **relationships** between your entities are a big part of Core Data, and in the preceding example, there are no relationships at all.

Also, because the main action is searching, it looks like it's not going to be in your app data layer but rather a dedicated database to dig in.

Core Data performs best when its role is to be your app data layer and serve the app business logic.

In this case, it is better to use a database like SQLite.

Design Your Data Model

Okay, so this step is not related solely to Core Data.

You should design your data model no matter what data framework you plan to implement.

This is the part where you need to understand your app business but mostly understand how to take an existing app and design your data model.

Sometimes your app is not in a state where your data model is clear. Sounds weird?

Anything can happen in apps that have existed for a few years and had different iterations that caused their app data model to be a complete mess.

For example, some apps use JSON files to store different data types and SQLite for others.

This situation can happen due to different development teams that worked on the project and decided to "start a refactor" and haven't finished.

Another aspect of data model issues can be its **compatibility with the UI screens**.

The main goal of your data model is to serve the UI. At this stage, your current local data structure may not be suitable for your business logic and the UI.

Replicating that problem with Core Data is not a good idea, and you should think about how to take the existing structure and transform it into something more practical.

Implementing Core Data

After you understand your needs and have a basic understanding of your data model, your next move will be **to implement** Core Data.

That is a scary and sensitive step, and to verify this move is going faultless, you need to build a plan that transfers your app to work with Core Data.

The first step is to ensure **you have enough tests** covering the significant parts of apps, focusing on integration tests.

After that, you need to decide your strategy. Some directions to consider are as follows:

- You can decide to implement **only new entities** in Core Data while transferring old entities overtime. This has a lot to do with how your app evolves and how the relationships between your entities are connected.

- Migrating all current data to Core Data is probably the fastest way of working, but it is also hazardous. The problem, in this case, is not only migrating a significant amount of data but also **changing how your business logic works**.

- Another option would be **building a custom data store**. A custom data store preserves the current persistent store you work with, but requires you to change your business logic to work with Core Data. That can be a step toward completing Core Data migration in the future.

The preceding options list can provide you with some ideas for dealing with this complicated mission.

It is also derived from the current state of the project, resources, and time.

Where to Go from Here

It's a big book, but it's not the bible. You must always doubt what you are reading.

Explore Core Data further by reading documentation, watching WWDC video sessions, and testing the framework yourself.

Implement Core Data responsibility slowly and consistently according to your needs.

Remember that Core Data is a tool. A great tool! But it is not the goal – your app quality is the goal.

Thanks

It has been a pleasure for me to write this book and to unleash Core Data with you. I hope you had a great reading, and thanks!

Index

A

Accent, 124
Adding methods, 56
Aggregate operators, 118, 133, 136
Album entity, 14, 25, 45, 50, 214
Album entity mapping, 246, 247
albumID, 14, 69, 220
Album-to-song relationship, 71
ANY operator, 136
App container, 268, 298
App Delegate, 30, 32, 142, 295
App extensions, 298
App group, 299–301, 305
Apple Developer Portal, 300
Apple Instruments, 220
Apple's search engine, 290
App models, 11
Arrangement limitation, 77
Atomic stores, 265, 266, 268, 269,
    277, 283, 286
Attributes, 39, 40
   Boolean, 42
   date, 42
   number, 41
   string, 42
   types, 40
   URI, 43

Attributes inspector, 58
   additional settings, 62
   default value, 59, 60
   Optional setting, 58, 59
   scalar type, 60–62
   transient, 59
Auto-generating code, 53
Automatic process, 29

B

Backend server, 3
Batch faulting, 202–204, 227
Batch saving, 217, 218
beginUpdates() method, 163, 164
BETWEEN operator, 127
Binary Data, 43, 123
Business object, 150

C

Cascade rule, 75, 76
Case-insensitive searches, 215–217
Category/Extension, 56
cellForRow function, 159
Child contexts, 111
   create, 112
   sync with parent, 112, 114

X, Y, Z

xcdatamodeld file, 16

Xcode

relationship, 70

configure, 72

destination, 71

entities, 85

inverse, 71

name, 71

type, 73

user interface, 50

wizard, 30

XML store types, 23

Printed in the United States
by Baker & Taylor Publisher Services